Guide

The Force
of Destiny
La Forza
del Destino
Verdi

Josephine Barstow as Leonora in 1983 in the ENO production by Colin Graham, designed by David Collis (photo: Andrew March)

Preface

This series, published under the auspices of English National Opera and The Royal Opera, aims to prepare audiences to evaluate and enjoy opera performances. Each book contains the complete text, set out in the original language together with a current performing translation. The accompanying essays have been commissioned as general introductions to aspects of interest in each work. As many illustrations and musical examples as possible have been included because the sound and spectacle of opera are clearly central to any sympathetic appreciation of it. We hope that, as companions to the opera should be, they are well-informed, witty and attractive.

The Royal Opera is very grateful to The Baring Foundation for making possible the publication of this Guide to *The Force of Destiny*.

Nicholas John
Series Editor

23

The Force of Destiny
La Forza del Destino

Giuseppe Verdi

Opera Guide Series Editor: Nicholas John

*Published in association with
English National Opera and The Royal Opera
and assisted by a generous donation
from The Baring Foundation*

John Calder · London
Riverrun Press · New York

First published in Great Britain, 1983, by
John Calder (Publishers) Ltd,
18 Brewer Street,
London W1R 4AS

and

First published in the U.S.A., 1983, by
Riverrun Press Inc.,
175 Fifth Avenue,
New York, NY 10010

Copyright © English National Opera 1983 and The Royal Opera 1983

War and Peace © Peter Conrad 1983

The Music of 'The Force of Destiny' © Richard Bernas 1983

'That Damned Ending' © Bruce A. Brown 1983

'The Force of Destiny' English translation by Andrew Porter © G. Ricordi & Co. 1983

ALL RIGHTS RESERVED

BRITISH LIBRARY CATALOGUING IN PUBLICATION DATA
Verdi, Giuseppe
    The force of destiny.—(Opera guide; 23)
    1. Verdi, Giuseppe. Fuerza del sino, La
    2. Operas—Librettos
    I. Title   II. Piave, Francesco-Maria
    III. John, Nicholas   IV. Series
    782.1'092'4   ML410.V4

ISBN 0-7145-4007-2

Library of Congress Catalogue Card Number 83-045246

John Calder (Publishers) Ltd., English National Opera and The Royal Opera House, Covent Garden Ltd., receive financial assistance from the Arts Council of Great Britain. English National Opera also receives financial assistance from the Greater London Council.

Typeset in Plantin by Margaret Spooner Typesetting, Dorchester, Dorset

Printed and bound in Great Britain at The Camelot Press Ltd, Southampton

Contents

List of Illustrations

The photographs by Angus McBean are © Harvard Theatre Collection and those by Houston Rogers are Crown Copyright.

War and Peace

Peter Conrad

Ever since the 1862 première, when the critic of *Russki Mir* derided the absurdity of its libretto, *The Force of Destiny* has been admired for its music and deplored as drama. Assuming it to be incoherent, those who stage it feel entitled to edit or rearrange it. The 1950s Met. production, until John Dexter took responsibility for it, used to omit the scene at the Hornachuelos inn; often the rabble-rousing interventions of Preziosilla are excised, or else she's retained — as by Joachim Herz in his 1981 Welsh National Opera version — as an ideological caricature, being made to behave like a militaristic maenad. Herz also, to make the work more philosophically acceptable to himself, exchanged Verdi's conciliatory La Scala ending (1869) for the original St Petersburg conclusion (1862), where Alvaro refuses religious consolation and hurls himself over a cliff to a nihilistic death. Verdi has not often been allowed the benefit of the doubt: what might he have meant in this idiosyncratic work? Why, for instance, does he prefer the subtitle of the Duke of Rivas's play *Don Alvaro, o La Fuerza del Sino*? Why did he select a drama in which the action digresses across Europe at apparent random, in which first Alvaro and then Leonora disappear from the drama for acts at a time, and why did he diversify the narrative further by adding scenes from a completely different play by another playwright (*Wallensteins Lager* by Schiller)? We ought at least to credit him with dramatic intentions; and if we do, the opera can be seen to be one of his boldest constructions.

It is less an account of individual fates than a demonstration of the working of history — Verdi's equivalent to Berlioz's *Les Troyens* (*The Trojans*, 1864) and Wagner's *Ring* (1876). The title, under which all the accidents and misunderstandings of the drama are subsumed, is more than a cliché. It could be paraphrased as 'The Will of History'. The nineteenth century was convinced of a motorised propulsion in history. Mind, as Comte proclaimed, was on the march; dynamoes and their driven energy had invaded the static and eternal cathedral; our only freedom lay in the recognition of this necessity — our harried and hustled existence in time. What earlier centuries had understood as a religious providence was interpreted by the positivist nineteenth century as a natural impetus, scientifically harnessed in the turbines which so thrilled the contemporary American philosopher, Henry Adams. History had been accelerated by such miracle-working engines. One symptom of this overdrive was the cult of coincidence. Dickens wonders at such chances, which almost mystically ordain the action of his novels; Alvaro in *Forza*, telling Carlos he owes his life *'al caso'* ('to fortune') or that *'il destino'* killed the Marquis, is superstitiously alarmed by them.

In the overture with which in 1869 Verdi replaced the terse St Petersburg prelude, he turns his orchestra into a propulsive machine like Adams's turbines or Dickens's railway. It announces, in this blatant speeding-up of the motif associated with Leonora's flight, an impending and inescapable volition, which constrains all of us and keeps us exhaustingly on the move. The characters of *Forza* have no wills of their own. By their monastic retirements, Leonora and Alvaro solemnise a renunciation of will. Everything which happens to them is unintentional, cruelly coincidental: they are history's

7

Design by Carlo Ferrario for the première at La Scala of the 1869 version: the Inn

hapless victims. Wagner and Berlioz anatomise in Siegfried and Enée (Aeneas) an epic heroism which must affront its destiny no matter what human damage it causes along the way. These characters are the revolutionary mid-wives of history. Siegfried breaks Wotan's spear, Enée abandons Didon (Dido), who wants to detain him in Carthage when his fanatical vocation urges him on to the founding of Rome. *The Force of Destiny*, compassionately human, laments the violence of this indeflectible will. Though it approximates to the epic form of the works of Wagner and Berlioz, it rejects their morality. Leonora and Alvaro seek the peace of an exemption from history. Two opposite modes of life contend in *Forza*: the belligerence of epic against the cloistered solitude of confessional monologue; opera, with all its gaudy theatricality, against requiem.

The force of destiny compels drama as well as history. Drama is necessarily predestined. Aristotle insisted on the unity of time and place in plays: the stage is a room from which there can be no exit. This is the trauma of Verdi's first Shakespearean hero, Macbeth, who cannot outrun the consequences of his acts. History is the nightmare he is trying to escape; drama, with its foreclosing time and foreshortening space, adopts the shape of that nightmare. No work could be more flagrantly disunified, in Aristotle's sense, than *The Force of Destiny*, yet though it roams across Europe the drama is too claustrophobic and confining to allow the characters liberty from their pasts. Carlos catches up with his prey. The Verdi who mistrusts the callousness of those epic men of destiny (opportunists like the ambitious Radamès in *Aida*) also questions the determinism of drama, motivated and motorised by the thrustful human will, and he manages, after all, to free his characters from it. Leonora and Alvaro find a peace apart in seclusion, and death.

In the double plot of *Forza*, Verdi pays homage to Shakespeare (by way of Schiller, whose *Wallenstein's Camp* is a source for the military episodes). In the double-plotted Shakespearean history plays, the tragic preoccupations of the king are ignored by his feckless comic subjects, led by Falstaff. The demotic population of *Forza*, intent on keeping itself fed, warm, alive and in business, also doesn't heed the tragic imperatives of drama. No fatality can

8

Design for the final scene of the same production (Museo Teatrale alla Scala)

impose on Preziosilla, Trabuco, Melitone and the others, who wander and amuse themselves at will, profiting from whatever occasion presents itself to them. They behave less like the doomed internees of drama than the meandering, unflustered characters of nineteenth-century novels. Like Micawber, they can be relied on to be everywhere and always the same. This reflects indeed another of the great oppositions in *Forza*: the difference between the drama and the novel; between Rivas's play and the narrative of *I Promessi sposi* (*The Betrothed*) by Verdi's revered contemporary, Manzoni. For whereas the nineteenth-century drama insists on the velocity and wilfulness of history, hurtling ever ahead, the novel can afford reassuringly to ignore it or live it down, stressing life's calm continuance not the crises of politics. Novels, more interested in peace than in war, represent the century's great battles as confused, unintelligible hugger-muggers. Stendhal's Fabrice in *Le Rouge et le Noir* staggers through the muddle of Waterloo, fails to catch sight of Napoleon, and only discovers when he buys a newspaper after the event what the occasion meant; Thackeray omits the battle itself from *Vanity Fair*, and describes Jos Sedley's hasty decampment from Brussels; Pierre in *War and Peace* is a bemused spectator at Borodino.

Because of the contradiction within it between the imperative tempo of history and the longing for rest and safety, the stasis of introspection — that interior regime which the monastery makes a sacred rule — *The Force of Destiny* has two incompatible rhythms. The overture urges Leonora on her way, but throughout the first scene she hesitates and procrastinates. Curra fusses over the preparations for elopement, telling Leonora they'll get away quicker if she helps, while Alvaro describes his waiting, impatient horses. Leonora, however, dreads the itineracy of the life into which she will be cast adrift. She orders Curra to stop, and begs Alvaro to delay their departure. Already she is yearning for a different order of existence: a mystic quiet and reclusion possible only outside history and drama. In the second act, these clashing rhythms are institutionalised in two symbolically different locations, the inn and the monastery. Like an airport departure lounge, the inn sums up the transit and the transitoriness of history. Everyone will turn up there

Design for Act Two scene two by Edoardo Marchioro for the 1927 Scala production (Museo Teatrale alla Scala)

sooner or later, though no-one communicates with anyone else. It's a non-place, really: a way-station or staging-post en route to somewhere else, an incident in an incessant mobility. The scene's refrain — on which the disputatious groups of pilgrims and profiteers, hunters and quarry, muleteers and students agree — is the injunction of its final line, *'Andiam, andiam, andiam'* ('We'll go!'). Verdi orchestrates here the divisive double-plottedness and chaotic simultaneity of history. Everything is happening at once as the scene begins, and the collision of contrary purposes begets ensembles which are rehearsals of warfare, sometimes jocose (in Preziosilla's teasing of Carlos), sometimes more threatening (when Carlos bullies Trabuco). Preziosilla exults in the affray. Her hymns to battle advertise a romantic orthodoxy: energy to her is eternal delight. Other characters plead for an end to involvement in this historical struggle. It's significant that Leonora's presence in the scene is so fugitive and unemphatic. Her only moment of vocal splendour comes when she anonymously incorporates herself into the chorus of pilgrims and joins their prayer. As during her investiture in the monastery chapel, she no longer demands the vocal monopoly which is so dear to the operatic ego; content to be a member of a community and a choir, she has resigned from the fraught individuality of dramatic character. Her choice is comically reflected at the inn when Trabuco remarks that he's in purgatory while Carlos importunes him; he hopes he may be permitted to advance to Heaven.

In contrast with the inn, at the monastery all journeys (and time itself) terminate. Leonora on reaching it declares *'Son giunta'* ('I'm safe here!'). Whereas for Preziosilla, urging migration to Italy, motion is the principle of life, for Leonora arrival, not the journey, is what matters. And as her refuge from the warfaring contentions of drama and history, the monastery also

Rosa Ponselle (Leonora), Enrico Caruso (Alvaro) and José Mardones (Father Guardiano) at the Met. on the occasion of Ponselle's Met. debut on November 15, 1918. (photo: Ida Cook Collection)

affords her a retreat from the opera. Once she's inducted into it, opera — passionately profane, extravagantly worldly — reverts to something like 'sacra rappresentazione' (sacred performance) from which, in the Renaissance, it derived. Every Verdi opera looks forward to his *Requiem* (1873); every Verdi heroine who's oppressed by the turmoil of the world, like Aida beside the Nile,

Claudia Muzio as Leonora (Museo Teatrale alla Scala)

or Amelia beneath the gibbet, or the praying Desdemona, anticipates the soprano of the *Requiem* who, lifted out of the particularities of drama, implores peace in the *'Libera me'* on their collective behalf. In the second scene of its second act, *Forza* seems already to have attained the sacredness and the abstraction of the *Requiem*. That scene effectively commemorates Leonora's passage into another world, so that her reappearances in the fourth act are like post-mortem apparitions. *'Pace, pace'* is the lament of a soul perambulating in purgatory; when she emerges from her hermitage, Alvaro thinks her a spectre. One of the undead, she is at last granted the mercy of an actual expiry.

As she renounces the confusion of history, drama yields to a detached recapitulation of itself, as if the freed soul were dismissively remembering the disasters and distress which assailed it during its entombment in a body. After the opening scene, nothing of consequence occurs in *Forza*. Characters spend their time instead remembering it and seeking extenuation for it. Thus Carlos's narrative at the inn; Leonora's agitated recitative at the monastery, her confession to Father Guardiano, and her re-traversal and expiation of that past in her last act soliloquy; Alvaro's meditation on his early life in his aria at Velletri. At the monastery, Leonora wills herself out of history and drama. Alvaro is condemned to go on living in them, but he treats the world as a

12

Francesco Merli who sang Don Alvaro at La Scala in 1929 (Museo Teatrale alla Scala)

purgatory and practices his own mode of abstraction from it, wandering through the action at Velletri like a ghost. The clarinet soliloquy which introduces him there is his equivalent to Leonora's peace: a pastoral state — hence its depiction by a woodwind — of humility and quietus. So accidental and irrelevant has action now become that the battle can occur, revved-up and telescoped, off-stage, and it's quickly ended by the musical modulation which reports on Alvaro's apparent death. For him, war's purpose is the attainment of a peace which doesn't mean victory (as it does to Preziosilla) but easeful death.

The Force of Destiny seems to stop half-way through, and only reluctantly resumes. That structural hiccup expresses its discontent with drama. Actions are involuntary spasms, essentially meaningless. Wordsworth makes this, in *The Borderers*, a rule of romantic literary form:

> Action is transitory — a step, a blow,
> The motion of a muscle — this way, or that —
> 'Tis done, and in the after-vacancy
> We wonder at ourselves like men betray'd:
> Suffering is permanent, obscure and dark,
> And shares the nature of infinity.

He might be describing *Forza* where, instead of a step or blow, the contingent action is the misfiring of a pistol. A formulation like Wordsworth's disrupts drama, in which action supposedly begets reaction. Instead, Verdi's characters disavow the initial action, happening as it did against their wills, and seek a respite from reaction. Leonora reaches that suffering inertia at the end of the second act. Then at Velletri, almost in spite of itself, the drama continues. History can't be arrested yet; the family dispute is now embroiled in a larger international strife. Though Leonora's dramatic course has ended, Alvaro — who dominates the second half of the work as she had done the first — can't retire from the mortal fight. His half is about this enforced, resented resumption of the drama. Friendship with Carlos recalls him to life, or to an illusion of it: he and his enemy introduce themselves using aliases, as if the existence they share is an imposture. *'All'armi'* ('To battle!') is their cry of dramatic engagement, and they briefly join in Preziosilla's enthusiasm for the volatile comings and goings of this world. But that rebirth only prolongs their earthly affliction. Alvaro's 'salvation' by the surgeons is celebrated by Carlos because now he can have the pleasure of killing him personally. The reveillé which rouses the soldiers makes the same point. It's a summons back to the routine of living (not a brazen announcement of an after-life, like the trump of doom in the *Requiem*).

Carlos embodies the frantic, vengeful energy of the overture. He is the dual impetuosity of drama and history, and his rebarbative function is to serve as a dramatic antagonist, to keep going an action which Leonora and Alvaro (who follows her into monastic seclusion after the first skirmish) wish to still. Hence the taunts by which he provokes Alvaro into duelling with him. Like Leonora in the fourth act, Alvaro will consent to return to life only if he's guaranteed, as a reward for his pains, the certainty of death. Their refrain as they hurl themselves into the duel is *'Morte! morte! morte!'*. Carlos thrives in dramatic time, in crisis and catastrophe, while Leonora and Alvaro both choose to remove themselves into an eternity where nothing happens. There's a corresponding contrast between the bogus fortune-telling of Preziosilla, who supplies the conscripts with wish-fulfilling fantasies about their futures, and Father Guardiano's prohibition, in his duet with Leonora, on reading into the future. Guardiano is a necessary presence in the final scene, because he must over-rule any misunderstanding of the end as a dramatic dénouement, interpreting Leonora's death as an ascent to God and enjoining Alvaro to prayer, not imprecation. Even Melitone learns, in the course of the work, this renunciatory wisdom. When Leonora arrives at the monastery, he's anxious to overhear her story and teased by the dramatic possibilities of scandal; later, denouncing the reprobates at Velletri, he's a changed man, and the puns in his aria of castigating patter alternate, like *Forza* itself, between sacred and profane, eternity and time, requiem and opera.

In its ambitious scope, *The Force of Destiny* is the one Verdi work which demands comparison with *Les Troyens* or the *Ring*; but the conclusions it reaches about history are profoundly different from those of Berlioz or Wagner. History's dynamo-like, destructive will is incarnated in the empire-building Enée or the sword-wielding Siegfried. Verdi, however, proposes here a criticism and a pacification of that activist will, and of the fatal factitious dramas it generates.

Montserrat Caballé as Leonora at La Scala in the 1977/78 season (Teatro alla Scala: Archivio Fotografico)

La Scala 1965/66: Carlo Bergonzi as Alvaro (Teatro alla Scala: Archivio Fotografico)

Designs by Nicola Benois for the 1949 production at La Scala

The Music of 'The Force of Destiny'

Richard Bernas

By the time he started work on *The Force of Destiny*, Verdi had some twenty-two operas behind him. The majority belonged to that period of quick turnover and mixed results he called his 'galley years' but each of the new operas leading up to *Forza*, *The Sicilian Vespers* (1855), *Simon Boccanegra* (1857) and *A Masked Ball* (1859), broke new ground in one way or another. *Forza*'s chief contribution to this process is its great expansion of scale and intent. Only the succeeding *Don Carlos* rivals it in this respect and it is certainly the most ambitious of Verdi's creations up to this point. *Forza* is an 'opera of ideas', rather than a work that follows the linear development of the characters.

The composer admitted that it was 'certainly something quite out of the ordinary'. And it is indeed out of the ordinary to conceive of a four-act opera which, for instance, drops the main thread of the action in order to present — three-quarters of the way through the work and lasting over 120 pages of 556 pages of full score — a collection of beggars, pedlars, recruits, soldiers, gipsies and priests who set out (but do not even explain) the state of society at the time, neither involving nor drawing moral commentary on the main characters. Such ambitions could aptly be described as Tolstoyan — it is an extraordinary coincidence that the opera was commissioned by the St Petersburg opera.

The impact of *Forza* in the theatre is cumulative, partly as a result of these dimensions, partly in spite of them. For underneath Verdi's wide-ranging dramatic ambitions, a firmly drawn set of musical cross-references holds the opera together. These references, of key, orchestration and melodic outline, are not the elaborate hypothetical intentions of Wagnerian drama. They do not seem to have been entirely predetermined by Verdi, but are rather the intuitive comprehension of an author whose unity of thought, execution and effect was highly developed.

When asked how he composed, Verdi explained: The idea comes to me in all its completeness, and above all I hear whether a certain note ought to be played by a flute or a violin. The difficulty is in writing it all down fast enough, and in being able to express the musical idea in the integrity in which it came to my mind.' If we examined *Forza* from a bibliographic viewpoint, forming an opinion of it through the history of its composition — and especially the various revisions it underwent — the analysis would be laborious, the conclusions possibly contradictory. For example, Carlos's aria *'Urna fatale'* (No. 20), which is dramatically vital both in terms of plot and personality, is sung in the same key (E major) as much else of his music; this is also the key of other related action, and of the Overture. Careful planning on the part of the composer could be presumed. But in fact *'Urna fatale'* was first written a semitone higher, in F. It was only brought down into line with much else of Carlos's music for the singer Luigi Colonnese at the première of the revised version at La Scala in 1869.

But speculation as to whether this afterthought was prompted by structural or practical considerations is unrewarding. By examining the 1869 score from the perspective of the audience, we can discover a great deal about how this opera is *heard*, rather than how it was composed; the impact it has in the theatre, how Verdi makes his points and how the audience receives them.

17

- key as revealing intent

A composer with a keen dramatic perception controls not just what the listener hears, but influences what he remembers through repetition of essential material. The choice of key (and consequently, of register) is important. It subtly aligns the memory with similar previous passages. Verdi's use of keys is pervasive enough in *Forza* to represent an index, a barometer, of the main characters' emotional status. Even when Leonora, Alvaro or Carlos are in disguise, it still reveals their intentions.

Leonora, Alvaro and Carlos

By looking at the first Act in some detail, we will discover how Verdi deploys these devices to illuminate his protagonists. The survey of his tactics in later Acts will then be that much easier.

After the elaborate, thematically-related Overture (best discussed retrospectively), the opera moves fast. Act One telescopes character exposition and crucial action (Alvaro's inadvertent killing of the Marquis of Calatrava, Leonora's father). An opening dialogue between Leonora and the Marquis is introduced, and disturbingly interrupted, by thin-sounding Es played by flute and clarinet in low register, a ghostly echo of the brassy unisons that punctuate the Overture.

Leonora's Romanza, *'Me pellegrina ed orfana'* ('Now I must leave my native land') introduces a passionate but equivocating young woman. It is in F major, nervously poised a semitone higher than the key of the Overture and opening conversation. And within that key it moves restlessly. (The opening phrase is harmonized with chords of F major and minor and D flat major, quite a way to travel before returning to F major.) An ascending solo cello defines points of tonal rest, but its speed and upward movement only add to the uneasy mood. Vocal rhythms move from smooth to disjunct as key phrases of the text are repeated.

If we compare this to the introductory aria of Verdi's earlier Leonora (in Act One of *Il Trovatore*, and also secretly waiting for her lover) we discover similar expansions — repetitions of the text and the music. But that calmer heroine's music develops in a continuous, contained flow. The later Leonora repeats her lines more impulsively, less smoothly connected with what has gone before. The contrast between her obligations to her father and to Alvaro couldn't be more clear; consider the palpitating figure that leads to the soft, tearful flow of the music at *'Ti lascio, ahimè, con lacrime, dolce mia terra'* ('I leave, alas, alas, in tears I leave my native country'). This is characterisation as vivid as it is precise.

The clatter of horses' hooves is graphically depicted by the orchestra. This accelerates the pace of the music alarmingly, paving the way for one of Verdi's more difficult tenor entries. Alvaro's aim is to sweep Leonora off her feet. If he jumps onstage and sings his expansive, rapid first lines just as Verdi indicated, he will succeed in doing the same to the audience.

In keeping with the compression of the Act, Don Alvaro soon presents the kernel of his musical personality. The tender, optimistic music of the line *'ma d'amor sì puro e santo'* ('But our love is pure and holy') repeated exactly and then extended with the completion of the sentence, features a rising figure composed of two fourths within the overall span of a minor sixth [2]. This figure is cited later, when all of Alvaro's hopes are lost, and the span of a sixth becomes the melodic profile of many of his, and Leonora's, key utterances. In this original form it is over almost before we can take it in.

Spanning a major sixth, Alvaro's *'Pronti destrieri'* ('Horses are waiting') [3] reinforces the melodic characterisation, as do some of the sighs that

one again Alvaro's melodious

Martina Arroyo (Leonora) and Charles Craig (Alvaro) at Covent Garden in 1973 (photo: Reg Wilson)

accompany Leonora's prevaricating speech (for example, at the height of her confused protesting, she pleads *'Io t'amo'* ('I love you') over a minor sixth). So within the space of a few minutes, Verdi has established Alvaro's musical character and linked it to Leonora's during the course of a fast-moving sequence of short musical numbers.

When finally won over, Leonora launches into *'Seguirti fino agl'ultimi confini della terra'* ('I'll follow you through all the world') [4] pitched a semitone higher than her opening Romanza, and in the same key as Alvaro's declaration *'ma d'amor'*. Though there is no strict harmonic relationship between the Romanza and the start of this duet, there is undoubtedly a sonorous one; the key sounds that much brighter — Leonora's former worries have lifted. The relentless brass line and off-the-beat accompaniment further support this emotional charge. Heard in isolation, it might seem a superficial piece, but its impetuosity is reinforced masterfully by the context. It can also convey some tenderness if the singers obey Verdi's quieter dynamic injunctions as much as they revel in his exclamations.

A timpani rumble slightly delays the progress of the music, but in conventional operatic terms we are set for a triumphal conclusion and exit. The whole orchestra suddenly sits on a note quite unrelated to the key of G flat. With hindsight, it is not surprising that it is an E (the key of the Overture and opening). In the theatre, it sounds as if the orchestra had pulled the rug out from under the singers' feet; we experience a jolt no matter how familiar the music may be. The Marquis rushes in and the Act swirls to its conclusion. The music is propelled by the opening figure of the Overture (which spans a minor sixth at its conclusion) and is in C sharp minor, the relative minor, the dark side, of E major.

In the next scene we discover the third protagonist, Leonora's brother, Don Carlos de Vargas, amidst the bustle of the inn of Hornachuelos. Disguised as a student and friend of Carlos, he relates the Vargas tragedy from the viewpoint of a sympathetic observer, convinced of the necessity of avenging the Marquis's murder. His ballata, *'Son Pereda, son ricco d'onore'* ('I'm Pereda, a hard-working student') [6] starts affably, *con eleganza*, in A major, a key closely related to E major. When the student sings of Alvaro's escape from vengeance, the mood becomes more intense. Although Carlos's vocal line does not alter in style or diction, the orchestra is infiltrated by obsessively repeated, dogged-sounding short musical figures. The accompaniment moves to an E pedal, over which strings seethe and boil. An abrupt, heavily scored crescendo of frightening violence almost gives his disguise away. He realizes that his emotions are getting the better of him, and finishes the tale in the smooth manner he started it. These few bars of orchestral and emotional intensification prepare us for the hostility and diligence of his subsequent actions. The opening and closing tableaux of this scene are in A (first minor, then major), so it is apt that Carlos-as-Pereda should sing in that key. And it is no accident that when his emotions threaten to overturn his disguise, it should be expressed by music in the dominant of A, E major.

Leonora makes a short appearance at the inn. Most of her lines are of a simple declamatory nature and her chief musical contribution is to the ensemble prayer initiated by off-stage pilgrims, singing in antique-sounding harmonies in the key of G minor. Her soprano soars over the conventional pieties of the other travellers. Her pleas for divine mercy are that much more immediate. And their fulfilment occurs in the second scene of the Act.

This opens with the second of Leonora's great solos, *'Madre, pietosa vergine'* ('Virgin, look down and comfort me') [7]. This is pitched at B minor/major, a key (again) closely related to E, but also related to the key of her ecstatic duet with Alvaro in Act One. The breathless yet calm accompaniment is marked *come un lamento* and Verdi takes the trouble to emphasize the alternation between the fifth and minor sixth degrees of the scale of B minor with solo flute and clarinet colouring the faster moving violins.

The placing of the minor and major sixth in this scene and in Act Three, so strategic and psychologically illuminating, is too extensive to examine at length here. Some salient examples are listed on the facing page.

The ensuing duet with Father Guardiano has an extraordinary harmonic groundplan: it oscillates between the keys of F, evoking Leonora's Act One Romanza, and E, the key that becomes more strongly associated at each appearance with the black destiny of the house of Calatrava. This is the most concentrated example in the opera of Verdi's use of key to index emotional states. The fluctuation is harmonically extreme, and it is not only the outcome of, but related in keys to, the events of the first Act. Despite the lack of stage activity, the level of intensity in this duet is great. Leonora sings with the contrasts of rhythm and phrase that distinguished her Romanza, but here her diction is more extravagant [9]. Father Guardiano, by far the most sympathetic of Verdi's clerics, is firmly, soberly drawn. His vocal line consists of simple arpeggios of chords, or stepwise melodic movement. There are a few wide leaps, and when they occur they are used to reinforce a harmonic close [10, 11].

Music Examples

These examples show the distinctive leaps of a sixth which occur throughout the score.

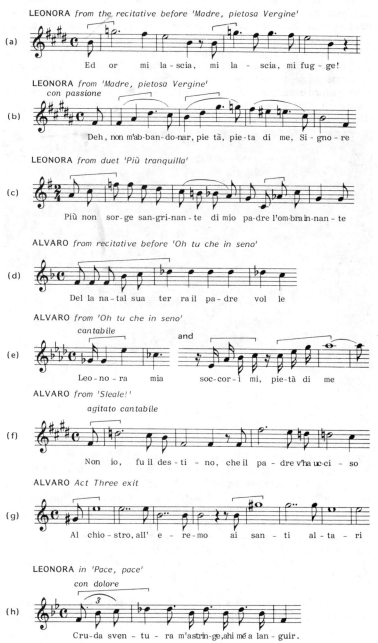

21

Up to this point, the pace of the opera has not let up. The ceremonial finale of the Act, in Alfred Einstein's phrase 'a climax of pure opera, at once theatre and exaltation'*, owes much of its sense of release to its static and ritualistic character. As with many of Verdi's rituals (for example, the priests' off-stage interrogation of Radames in *Aida*) a lot of the music moves in triptychs of phrases. Guardiano instructs the monks *'Il santo speco noi le schiudiamo'* ('The holy cave to him shall be opened') [14] with a simple vocal line which is then delivered twice more, each time a tone higher. The prayer, *'La Vergine degli Angeli'* ('The blessed Virgin pray for thee') [15] also has a triple phrase structure. First the chorus chants it; then Leonora sings it as a solo, accompanied by harp and a few woodwind; finally they join together for its last intonation. This last section of the Act is in G major, relating to and fulfilling the Prayer of the opening scene of the Act, when Leonora cried out for mercy.

Don Garrard as Father Guardiano in the 1981 Welsh National Opera production by Joachim Herz (photo: Julian Sheppard)

Here her soprano is, for the only time, calm and serene. With the gentle harp arpeggios and noble vocal line Verdi was, perhaps deliberately, evoking the style of Bellini in order to conjure up the certainties of a simpler age.

It is thrilling, too, to hear pre-echoes of the Manzoni Requiem (1874) as the monks curse anyone who might disturb Leonora's peace; and frightening to hear, just before they invoke the elements to scatter the ashes of any intruder, three quiet, unsettling Es played by solo horn.

As the next Act represents a striking change of location, so Verdi presents his characters within a new tonal frame. Three main 'genre' scenes — the opening gambling chorus, the dawn patrol's Ronda *'Compagni, sostiamo'* ('Take care now, be silent') and Preziosilla's concluding Rataplan — are in C major, a key we haven't heard much so far.

Alvaro's Recitative and Romanza *'O, tu che in seno agli angeli'* ('High in the realms of paradise') [16] is prefaced by a brooding clarinet solo which

---

* *Music in the Romantic Era* (London, 1947)

22

starts with a fragment of the theme *'ma d'amore'* from Act One, but in a tonality (F major) a semitone flatter than its original form. References to Leonora and her father are reinforced by sixths (examples (d) and (e) on page 21). Verdi chose A flat as the key of Alvaro's only solo. This sonority will impart a distinctive colour to his participation in the duets with Carlos.

But they sing the first of these three great numbers while they are both concealing their identities. In keeping with the tactic established in Act Two scene one (Carlos-as-Pereda), *'Solenne in quest'ora'* ('In death's solemn moment') [17] is set in the key of the surrounding scene (C minor and major), the tonal frame of this military Act. But the tonality does not prevent Alvaro's musical persona from emerging, as it surely does in the minor sixth on the phrase *'giurarmi dovete far pago un mio voto'* ('oh grant me one favour'). The pessimistic mood of the duet is enhanced by the tread of *pizzicato* cellos and

Act Three in the 1951 Glyndebourne production (photo: Angus McBean)

basses, the lugubrious colour of the bassoons and divided violas without the sweetness of violins.

Carlos's two-part aria of discovery — both of Alvaro's identity and the depths of his own rage — is set in E major, both the central key of his role and the predominant key of the opera. The aria is also located at the central point of the drama. His obligations as an honourable man, the temptation to break his word, seemingly forced on him by Destiny, are expounded in a purposeful but still elegant vocal line. The coloratura extensions of phrase at the close and the ambitious cadenza would suit the chivalrous Count di Luna (in *Il Trovatore*), had Verdi allotted that character any pensive moments. Yet the ominous French horn Es that lead the baritone into the words *'un giuro è sacro per l'uomo d'onore'* ('All vows are sacred to men of honour') are, as we have seen, characteristic of *Forza*.

The cabaletta, *'Egli è salvo'* ('Ah! He is safe!') has been compared, with its vigour and bluntness, to earlier Verdi. But much of its ferocity stems from the unexpected holds on the (upbeat) beginnings of phrases, as if Carlos's joy in his vengeance is so great that he can barely utter another word. As with the

23

more athletic of Alvaro's outbursts, any singer that can deliver an uncut performance of this hard-headed, thrusting music without spoiling the rhythms to accommodate extra breaths will inevitably give a vivid picture of the protagonist.

The second duet of Act Three is provoked by Carlos revealing his identity to Alvaro and challenging him to a duel. Alvaro exclaims: *'Sleale!'* ('Disloyal!') [19]. Carlos takes the initiative, so the music moves breathlessly in E major. When Alvaro pleads with him for reconciliation, he does so in his own sonority of A flat *'No, d'un imene il vincolo'* ('No, we'll fulfil that sacred vow') [20] and Carlos's rebuff is seconded by a typically obsessive repeated figure, gruffly delivered by violas and cellos (*'Stolto!'* 'Madman!'). His oath to kill Leonora again gives Carlos the dramatic lead. The music rushes foward in E minor, accompanied by rising chromatic scales similar to the single ferocious explosion that revealed his anger in the middle of *'Son Pereda'*.

As the duel is interrupted, the tonality veers off in a surprising direction. Alvaro is left alone with his thoughts, and a simple A flat trill on the violins captures both his loneliness and dazed confusion. Woodwind chords swing through organ-like sonorities of C sharp minor to E major as he swears — in phrases starting with minor and major sixths (example (g)) — to end his days in a monastery. But these harmonies, which reverse the closing and opening

ENO, 1983: Don Carlos (Neil Howlett) and Alvaro (Kenneth Collins) swear friendship (photo: Andrew March)

24

ENO, 1983: Don Carlos (Neil Howlett) goads Brother Raphael (Kenneth Collins) to a duel (photo: Andrew March)

tonalities of Act One, indicate to us that Alvaro's problems are only avoided, not resolved.

Again the music changes direction. We are prepared for another scene, but of a radically different kind. The stage is populated by all the 'low life' of a military camp and the shock after Alvaro's intense expression of despair has the alienating effect of Brechtian Epic Theatre.

There are many other instances of comedy and tragedy juxtaposed in Verdi's operas. Violetta dies while the carnival goes on outside; the entire dramatic apparatus of *A Masked Ball* sets up brilliant, comic conclusions to tragic, or potentially tragic, occurrences, only to reverse the procedure to devastating effect in the last scene. Victor Hugo's preface to his forgotten drama *Cromwell* summarizes this important feature of Romantic drama: 'The sublime added to the sublime makes for poor contrast and one has need of rest from everything, even beauty. It seems rather that the grotesque offers respite, a term of comparison, a departure point from which one mounts towards beauty, with a fresher and livelier perception.'

The variety of this ensuing scene in *Forza* is remarkable, even in comparison to Hugo's or Verdi's other achievements. Although it is naturalistic in its presentation, its location in the plot is surrealistic. (The composer Luigi Dallapiccola has observed that surrealism, not realism, is a fundamental condition of opera.)* This undeniably disturbing quality has always meant that the scene has been greeted with mixed reactions. Verdi noted that 'the vast, varied pictures which fill one half of the opera and which truly constitute the Musical Drama are ignored by the public. It is curious, and for our time, discouraging. Everyone cries out for Reform and Progress. In general, the public doesn't applaud and the singers only know how to be effective in Arias, Romanzas and Canzonettas! They do applaud the scenes of action for their reverberant noise, but only in passing, as the frame of the pictures. The relationship has been inverted — the frame has become the picture!'

* 'Words and Music in Italian 19th-century Opera' in *The Verdi Companion* (London, 1980)

25

When we return to Carlos in Act Four, he has once again caught up with Alvaro. His short soliloquy *'Invano Alvaro ti celasti al mondo'* ('In vain you seek to hide from the world, Alvaro') starts in a mood of deceptive calm, the key hovering a semitone above the E major that launches their third and last duet. During the declaration *'Col sangue sol cancella l'infamia ed il delitto'* ('By blood alone can we be cleansed') [25] the middle voices of the accompaniment, bassoons and cellos, move with familiar persistence. They link up with scales the broader intervals of Carlos's proud music, suggesting a speech that has often been rehearsed in anticipation of this final encounter. As before, Alvaro's attempts at reconciliation are cast in the key of A flat major (*'Le minnaccie, i fieri accenti'* 'All your fiery threats of vengeance') [26] with a vocal line full of minor sixths.

We are set for a repeat of the tonal pattern of *'Sleale'*, returning to the key of E, but instead, when Carlos insults Alvaro's ancestors, the tonality lurches sharply to A major, a calculated shock that indicates the vehemence of Alvaro's response.

The opening of the final scene is one of the finest examples of Verdi's profound humanity. The setting is described in the libretto as 'A mountain gorge between precipitous rocks, through which runs a little stream . . . It is sunset, growing slowly darker; later, brilliant moonlight.' Most composers would use this as the opportunity to paint an evocative musical prelude, but Verdi launches directly into the orchestral music associated with Leonora's calamity. Our attention is immediately focused on the person, not the setting.

'Pace pace' [27] superficially resembles the Bellinian *'La Vergine degli Angeli'* but it is more restlessly, chromatically, harmonized. The sonority is B flat major, the key of Alvaro's *'Pronti destrieri'* in Act One, so reinforcing the feeling of *'cruda sventura'* ('cruel misfortune') of which Leonora sings (example h).

The unhappy reunion of the lovers is swiftly set. We must marvel at the orchestral heartbeats that accompany her re-entry, mortally wounded. Harmonically related only by the pivotal woodwind wail of high Gs, these graphic orchestral figures have an impact far exceeding their basic means. The composer here becomes a sonic sculptor. The concluding trio presents Guardiano in a sympathetic light. His entry echoes a phrase of Leonora's Melodia and this minor sixth, presented in the key of A flat major, firmly but unobtrusively concentrates our attention on Alvaro. Verdi was worried that (unlike the trio that ends *Ernani*) the action of *Forza* ceases before the concluding trio even begins. But in the theatre, the solemnity and sense of hard-won, uneasy peace is heightened by the static stage picture, just as it is at the end of Act Two.

Leonora's dying music (*'Lieta poss'io precederti'* 'I gladly go to wait for you') is benevolence itself, simple diatonic music strongly contrasted with the heavy harmonies of Alvaro's complaint that he is condemned to life. Throughout the opera, she has been presented in the widest number of keys — her musical personality has fluctuated the most, since she has always been the victim of circumstance. This makes the harmonic simplicity of her death all the more moving. Verdi has skilfully avoided the trap of delivering a mere platitude.

Once Alvaro's identity is established in his Act Three Romanza, his musical image is fixed. His is the most demanding role in *Forza*, requiring great control equally in high-flying phrases (where the strength of Verdi's orchestration keeps the singer on a tight rhythmic leash), in long-breathed melodies, and in heavily scored *marcato* declamation. Moreover, none of these technical difficulties are of a spectacular sort. They serve the role, not the

Hervey Alan (Father Guardiano), Sena Jurinac (Leonora) and David Poleri (Alvaro) in the 1951 Glyndebourne production (photo: Guy Gravett)

singer. Verdi remarked that 'in *The Force of Destiny*, the singers don't have to know how to do "solfeggi" (singing exercises) but they must have soul, understand the words and express their meaning.' In its variety of writing and depth of characterisation, Alvaro is the Verdi tenor's equivalent of the bass Philip II in *Don Carlos*.

Carlos's part is scarcely less difficult, though it is shorter; his nobility is revealed, but only within an insistent and violent frame. As Alvaro's sonority is A flat, so Carlos's is E, and his role in the opera comes closest to embodying the power of destiny which overrules the protagonists' lives.

The Overture

Viewed from the musical perspective of these characters the Overture takes on a significance it lacks on the concert platform. By linking material that, in the opera, is separated by scenes or Acts ([1], [13], [27] and example (b) figure prominently), Verdi emphasizes their common melodic stamp — the minor or major sixth. This is not done to tell a story any more than to draw a moral. No good dramatic composer would do that before the curtain rose. But the Overture primes the audience's ears for these connections, and it is launched by those brassy, stentorian Es that echo all the way to the Third Act.

Melitone, Preziosilla, the Orchestra and Chorus

With the exception of Father Guardiano, we have avoided discussion of the other characters so far, since the musical inter-relationship of the three main protagonists demanded concentrated attention. Melitone cannot be ignored;

he appears in three scenes and each one is a remarkable thumbnail sketch. In Act Two scene two he is an uncaring and thus comic foil to Leonora's desperation, singing in wide intervals, declaiming his words asymmetrically with a pedant's urge to underline. For the first time, Verdi makes use of unexpected intervals to generate humour, as in Melitone's parting line: *'E se non torna, buona notte'* ('And if I don't come back, goodnight sir'). A sign of how quickly this personality is established is the vividness of his silent appearance when Father Guardiano summons him later in the scene. Although the orchestra only plays a fragment of his music, that is enough to enable him to dominate the action for a brief moment.

During the encampment scene, Melitone's sermon to the troops renounces the *buffo* diction of his first appearance and employs a more Heroic style. Such lines as *'Tutti, tutti cloaca di peccati'* ('You are all of you sinks of profanation'), proud *legato* phrases pitched near the top of the baritone register (significantly higher than Melitone's Act Two *tessitura*), would not sound out of place

Owen Brannigan (Melitone) preaches the sermon in the 1951 Glyndebourne production that toured to the Edinburgh Festival (photo: Angus McBean)

coming from a Simon Boccanegra. This is such a contrast with what we've heard before that it sounds doubly ridiculous. Verdi later exploited this tactic to great effect in Falstaff's 'honour' monologue.

In Act Four scene one Melitone is back to his Rossinian antics in an out-and-out comic *scena* berating the poor for their ingratitude. His subsequent duet with Father Guardiano could not show a greater contrast between the two clerics. True to character, Father Guardiano moves in conjunct steps, smooth and authoritative. Melitone leaps about, petulantly repeating his nobler companion's words with unconscious sarcasm. Verdi's setting of *'saranno i disinganni'* ('the world and its delusions') [24] is a model of this contrast. It also points the way to Iago's intentional sarcasm in *Otello*.

28

Renato Capecchi as Melitone in the 1962 Covent Garden production (photo: Houston Rogers)

As well as providing what Hugo called a 'departure point from which one mounts towards beauty', Melitone is an important reference point within the dramatic apparatus of *The Force of Destiny*. In this tale of separation, disguise and coincidence, he — very much a comic representation of the common man — is the only one of the characters to encounter all the other protagonists. Melitone reflects and comments on Leonora, Father Guardiano, Preziosilla, Alvaro and Carlos in turn, by his words or simply by his presence.

Richard Van Allan as Father Guardiano with Derek Hammond-Stroud as Melitone at ENO (photo: John Garner)

Preziosilla has, on occasion, a similar function. In Act Two scene one she operates as a contrasting personality to Carlos-in-disguise, much as Melitone does with Leonora in the next scene. Hers, however, is a difficult character to assess, not because of any psychological complexity but because of the style of her music. Alvaro's music is a Verdian foretaste of *verismo* tenor writing; aspects of Melitone anticipate both Iago and Falstaff; both Leonora and Carlos sing in the grand vocal style of Verdi's middle period. All this is familiar and coherent territory. But Preziosilla's music is modelled on that of the patriotic Isabella of Rossini's *The Italian Girl in Algiers* (1813); it requires the kind of rich, wide-ranging and agile voice that a low soprano or a high mezzo like Isabella Colbran, the first Semiramide, probably had, and this strangely old-fashioned aspect clearly sets her apart from the rest. It also explains why the character is so rarely sung well, and consequently adequately presented, in the theatre.

Indeed the original Preziosilla, Constance Nantier-Didier was, despite a French lightness and elegance reported by the Russian press, a useful rather than an outstanding artist, who did not completely satisfy Verdi's requirements.

Giulietta Simionato as Preziosilla at La Scala in the 1965/66 season (Teatro alla Scala: Archivio Fotografico)

Della Jones as Preziosilla in the 1983 ENO production (photo: Andrew March)

He toyed with the idea of re-setting the role as an unambiguously high soprano for a projected 1865 Paris revival, though this would have removed some of the striking Spanish flavour of the vivandière's low coloratura.

The structure of Preziosilla's music is also different. In a score that has only one designated aria (No. 20: Carlos's *'Urna fatale'*) and in which the tenor and soprano soliloquies are called Romanzas, Preziosilla sings the *couplets* of popular song. As in *opéra comique*, the melodies are simple, made up of short phrases, rarely developed, rhythmically jaunty and repetitive. Both *'Al suon del tamburo'* ('The drums gaily beating') [5] and *'Venite all'indovina'* ('Step up, my pretty maidens') rely on this easy-going format, bringing in the chorus to round off the verses in rousing fashion.

The instruments associated with her reinforce the popular image: Alvaro is prefaced by a solo clarinet; Leonora's Act One Romanza is introduced by solo cello; Preziosilla is, by contrast, italicized by the piccolo and side drum. The two piccolos which feature in *'Venite all'indovina'* are a particularly Rossinian touch — a colour which dominates the comic ensembles of *Cenerentola* (1817). The side drum is of course heard in *'Al suon del tamburo'*, but there the *pizzicato* strings provide at least as much colour. It really comes

Josephine Veasey as Preziosilla in the 1962 Covent Garden production by Sam Wanamaker (photo: Houston Rogers)

into its own in the famous Rataplan, where the side-drum is the only accompanying instrument for long stretches (Nantier-Didier created quite a stir by playing it herself).

This set piece shares some melodic fragments with a similar Rataplan in Donizetti's *The Daughter of the Regiment* (1840), and the onomatopœic chorus contribution of Pims, Pums and Rataplan-plan-plans has its precedent in the First Act finale of *The Italian Girl*. Yet the total effect of this curious number is novel and strangely Verdian. Preziosilla's athletic *coloratura* could be more efficiently presented by a solo cornet and, indeed, accompanied by the chorus's simple chords, the music recollects the vigorous *banda* passages that were such a feature of Verdi's Risorgimento operas. It is both Preziosilla's most popular song and her exit from the action. It is also the composer's fond, animated farewell to the populist certainties of his earlier works.

It is worth noting that *The Force of Destiny* was the first opera since *Nabucco* (1842) that Verdi was able to compose at his leisure. As the première was subject to a considerable delay, it was also orchestrated before rehearsals started, an entirely new practice for him. (*Rigoletto* (1851), for example, was orchestrated in only 40 days.) This does not result in an orchestral role as dominant or as sophisticated as that in *The Sicilian Vespers* (1856) or *A Masked Ball* (1859). Quite the opposite. The orchestra of *Forza* is a classic instance of Verdi's statement: 'Good orchestration is not variety and unique effects. Orchestration is good if it has meaning.' Aside of the solos or accompaniments already mentioned, the outstanding feature of the orchestra is the distribution of weight and colour to reinforce dynamics and to inflect phrasing.

Consider Alvaro's phrase '*il mondo inondi del suo splendor*' in '*Pronti destrieri*' (No. 2). It ends with the first climactic high B flat of Alvaro's part. The line begins softly, gradually enhanced by a timpani roll against high woodwind trills. A delayed entry of horns and tuba, which serves to thicken the texture, is capped by the brief entry of three trombones to fill out a single chord, for one bar only, under the tenor's highest note. Thus Verdi encourages and reinforces his singer, while enjoining him, via the tuba entry and all the bass instruments' descending scale, not to distend the phrase. The exact climax is precisely underlined by the three trombones joining the rest of the orchestra, so the conductor need not adjust dynamics or instrumentation in order to secure the musical and emotional meaning of the phrase. In Verdi's earlier operas, especially from *Nabucco* to *Il Trovatore*, passages can be found that are over-scored, clotted with doublings and difficult to realize in terms of the desired dynamics or phrasing. Here, everything sounds, each instrument contributes something vital and yet nothing draws attention away from the truthfulness of the vocal phrase.

The role of the Chorus in *Forza* is extensive and it is concentrated on the central acts of the opera. It does not appear at all in the opening or closing scenes. In the second Act the Chorus assumes two guises (guests at the inn, monks) yet it does not behave as a protagonist. Gradually, in Act Three, it takes a more animated part in establishing the atmosphere and location, as soldiers, gamblers, a dawn patrol, until in the extraordinary finale of the Act (the true Musical Drama in Verdi's estimation), animated by Preziosilla and Melitone, the Chorus assumes a greater individuality. Their musical material is here more fluent and less monumental, as sections such as the tenors and basses in '*Lorche pifferi e tamburi*' ('Drums and fifes are loudly sounding') (No. 23) break off to answer or contrast with the rest.

Verdi's individuation of the Chorus reaches its climax in the successive solos of beggars (basses), young recruits (altos) and vivandières (sopranos): a series of short, sharply contrasted snapshots of war-time life. Nowhere else in *Forza* does such a great variety of mood and texture occur in so short a space of time. And, as mentioned, the Chorus supplants the orchestra during the concluding Rataplan. Its status as a participant in the action is thus established, and it is further extended in the first scene of Act Four, when the chorus goads, cajoles and berates Melitone, transforming his *aria buffa* into a comic duet between two equally vivid characters.

This subsidiary activity is a necessary ballast to the high seriousness of Leonora and Alvaro. By lengthening *Forza*, Verdi greatly expanded and enriched its scope. It holds a particular place in audiences' affections as, in William Weaver's words, 'Verdi's boldest attempt to portray an entire, complex, contradictory world.' The composer's emotional architecture of shared intervals, tonalities and sonorities, never rigorously but poetically applied and reflecting the plight of Leonora, Alvaro and Carlos, is the underlying thread through this fabulous diversity.

33

The Revision of 'The Force of Destiny'

Chronology

1861	Composition
1862	Première in St Petersburg
1863	Performance in Madrid under Verdi's direction
1863/4	First attempts at revision
1865	Discussions for a French version for the Paris Opéra
1866	Performances in North and South America
1867	London première *Don Carlos* at the Paris Opéra
1868	Ricordi proposes a production at La Scala for early 1869, Ghislanzoni chosen to draft text changes
1869	Première of revised version at La Scala in February

A table showing the alterations made to the original version
of Acts Three and Four.

1862		1869	
		Act Three — *In Italy, near Velletri*	
No. 17	Scena and Romanza *Attenti al gioco* Male Chorus *Oh tu che in seno agli angeli* Alvaro	No. 16	
No. 18	Scena and Duettino *Amici in vita e in morte* Alvaro, Don Carlos, Male Chorus	No. 17	
No. 19	Scena and Battle *All'armi, all'armi!* Alvaro, Don Carlos, Surgeon, Male Chorus	No. 18	
		Change of Scene	
No. 20	Scena and Duettino *Solenne in quest'ora* Alvaro, Don Carlos, Surgeon	No. 19	
No. 21	Scena and Aria *Urna fatale del mio destino* Don Carlos, Surgeon	No. 20	
		Change of Scene	
—		No. 21	Ronda 'Patrol Chorus' *Compagni, sostiamo* Male Chorus
—		No. 22	Scena and 'Quarrel' Duet *Oh, tradimento! Sleale!* Alvaro, Don Carlos, Male Chorus

Act Four — *The neighbourhood of Hornachuelos*

Change of Scene

The final trio with Richard Van Allan, Kenneth Collins and Josephine Barstow at ENO, 1983 (photo: Andrew March)

'That Damned Ending'

Bruce Alan Brown

The Force of Destiny is unique among Verdi's operas because its revision was undertaken solely to correct defects in the plot, principally in the finale. In nearly every other case when the composer made changes in an earlier work, his main purpose was to modernise its musical language or to make it conform to the exigencies of a foreign theatre, or both. True, musical improvements resulted here also, but only because the need to change the plot had already provided an opportunity to do so. In the version of 1862 Don Alvaro fatally wounds Don Carlos onstage; the dying Carlos stabs Leonora; and as the monks, summoned by Leonora's alarm bell, hasten to the scene, Alvaro climbs a rocky bridge and, amid thunder and lightning, hurls himself to his death. The revised version ends with a trio in which Leonora (now wounded offstage) and the Padre Guardiano conjure Alvaro to accept his fate. In some ways it is remarkable that Verdi did revise the dénouement. The reviews of the first performance, in St Petersburg, had been largely favourable; in any case (if we believe Verdi) mere critics' opinions would hardly have moved him to rework so crucial a part of his opera as the finale. From his own testimony we know that (at least originally) he was satisfied with the ending provided in the play by the Duke of Rivas that was the source of his libretto. Yet some of the elements that most attracted him — the contrasts of plot and, especially, the 'force of destiny' itself — would return to haunt him almost from the moment the opera went before the public. His attempts over the next six years to tackle problems he or others perceived in the finale indicate that he must have been less immune to criticism than he professed to be — and susceptible, even when he was not himself convinced that the critics were right.

It is not unlikely that in casting Rivas's play into an opera Verdi was influenced by the preface that Faustino Sanseverino wrote to his Italian translation of the play. Sanseverino found the mixture of tragic and comic not a defect but a virtue, and in Don Alvaro he saw a wholly modern embodiment of the conflict 'between the spirit and the material, between a remnant of faith and scepticism, between the past and the future' — a figure sure to appeal to Verdi. In setting the subject Verdi even sharpened the contrasts with comic additions of his own.

Verdi repeatedly instructed Francesco Piave, his librettist, that 'the poetry can and must say everything that the prose says, in half the words'. The finale of Act Four takes over a great deal of actual text from the Italian translation; it was easy to do this because in its final scenes the play's dialogue moves forward far more quickly than in many loquacious scenes before. Here the changes are of the sort one would expect in a faithful adaptation of a spoken drama into an opera, where much textual subtlety is transferred to the music. In the finale Verdi opted for striking dramatic effect rather than musical beauty. There is no real 'number' after Leonora's aria. Nor had there been its spoken equivalent, a soliloquy, in the finale of the play. The successive *coups de théâtre* — recognition, homicides, suicide — do not permit this, and instead Verdi writes effective, but essentially functional, music — duelling noises, orchestral storming, highly charged recitative, and a chorus of monks which ends the opera with a horrified hush. The finale had, as Verdi wrote to Piave (November 20, 1861), 'nothing useless' and it moved 'rapidly to the end'.

Although in St Petersburg the opera's success was marred by some devotees of German music, Italy heard of the work mainly from the glowing account in the publisher Ricordi's *Gazetta Musicale di Milano* (November 23, 1862). In it there is, however, a well-aimed barb at the final duel which *'ends for lack of combatants'*. As Verdi moved on to Madrid to conduct the opera in the spring of 1863, another production was being mounted in Rome, without his supervision. Rather to his astonishment, the absurdities to which the plot was subjected by the Papal censorship did not prevent the performance from being applauded by the public. Nevertheless, the Roman paper *Eptacordo* (February 10, 1863) had serious reservations about the libretto, and especially about the 'three deaths onstage, censured also by the public'.

It is probably in reference to this production or to that in Reggio Emilia in April that Verdi first acknowledged complaints about the plot. On May 14 he wrote to Ricordi:

> They say [it] is too long, and that the public is frightened by so many deaths! Agreed: but once the subject is admitted, how is one to find another dénouement? The third act is long!! But where is the superfluous piece? The Camp Scene perhaps?

One of the elements attacked was particularly close to Verdi's heart — its motivating idea, the presence of which he saw as a hallmark of his new style. This letter to Ricordi concentrates rather more, however, on the poor singing and poor production at Reggio, factors that were significantly to colour Verdi's feelings about any proposed revisions. At first he had been tempted to take personal control of future performances so as to supervise these aspects and also the accuracy of the performing materials themselves; Verdi had seen when he arrived in Madrid how sloppily the parts had been prepared in Ricordi's copy workshop. He would then have the opportunity to make revisions in the score if he so wished — something he did regularly up to the end of his career. But the prospect of working with inadequate artists made Verdi lose enthusiasm for the proposed productions in Milan, Genoa, Naples, and even London. Ricordi patiently answered his protestations of 'do as you please with it' with arguments as compelling as the following (May 20, 1863):

> Once the opera is heard in Turin or Milan, not tortured nor massacred as other of your works have been, but done instead in such a way that its beauties are understood and enjoyed, why, then let the ill-wishers talk if they dare: *The Force of Destiny* will have conquered; and if later, going the rounds of other theatres, it will not always enjoy good fortune, one will have the right to condemn the performance, and the merit of the music will be invulnerable. — You will understand that in this affair, besides my esteem and friendship towards you, besides my love for the art, there enters also, somewhat, my own interest. Do you want me to let *The Force of Destiny* be massacred from theatre to theatre? Or do you want me to keep it in reserve, while waiting for the resurgence of the Italian theatre? I believe that this can be convenient neither to you nor to me.

For the moment, at least, Ricordi prevailed, and Verdi set himself seriously to the task of revising the opera.

By the end of October, he had written to Piave telling him that 'first of all it's necessary to think about the dénouement and find a way to avoid so many deaths' (October 30, 1863). He suggested that he should come to his home at Sant' Agata where they would work on the *'infernale scioglimento'* ('infernal dénouement') — henceforth Verdi hardly ever referred to the ending without this or some similar epithet.

The task would not seem to have been especially formidable; after all, in adapting Victor Hugo's *Hernani* Verdi had managed to reduce the number of deaths in the finale from three to one. But Piave found otherwise, writing in November that:

> I've found more than one way out, but I don't know which to decide on, and I find myself in a maze from which I confess I need your help to emerge without fear of breaking my head.

In July 1864 Verdi was still undecided, and no longer resolved to make future productions contingent upon revisions. Nor was he averse to discussing the problem and receiving suggestions from others. To Léon Escudier in Paris he write on July 29:

> the *Force of Destiny, Fatality*, cannot lead to the reconciliation of the two families: after making so much fuss the brother must avenge the death of his father (note too that he is Spanish), and never and again never can he consent to a marriage.
>
> De Lauzières [the future translator of *Don Carlos*] wanted to have a trio like that in *Ernani*, but in *Ernani* the action continues during the whole trio, and here the action ends just as the trio starts; thus it's useless to do it . . . Let's not think about this matter. I'm more mixed up than ever.

Evidently Verdi believed that more would need to be done than simply move the bloodshed offstage. Of course he did eventually opt for a trio but only when a new motive, which justified a lyrical ending, had been introduced.

Things were more or less at a standstill through the autumn and winter of 1864, although Ricordi was applying steady pressure to find a solution. Verdi wrote:

> It's not the piece of music that gives me trouble: that's an affair of two, three, four, five days; but it has to be changed in a way that's not worse than the old one.

Three times (September 8 and 23, and December 8) Verdi told Ricordi to let the opera be given as is. Ricordi replied (to the first of these letters) patronizingly but firmly that:

> it goes without saying that I will hold off letting it be performed until you've found an ending to your satisfaction. My interests in this case are too closely connected with yours for me not to want precisely that which you want.

At the end of 1864 Verdi enquired:

> Don't you have some poet, some literary friend who might be capable of finding an ending for this opera?

Ricordi suggested a number of poets, including Gutiérrez [from whose plays Verdi had fashioned *Il Trovatore* and *Simon Boccanegra*] and even the Duke of Rivas himself. But, answered Verdi:

> neither Gutiérrez nor the Duke would find anything. For a thousand reasons it's not right to turn to Ghislanzoni, nor to [Marcellino] Marcello, nor would Boito do in this case.

Although Ghislanzoni was the eventual choice, there were reasons (as we shall see) why Verdi was reluctant to work with him. He still considered writing to Rivas but turned also to his friend Count Opprandino Arrivabene. Early in 1865 Verdi communicated his pleasure that Arrivabene had not yet despaired of finding an ending, and outlined for him some of the features that it should have:

> It would be necessary . . . to leave in Leonora's *solo* scene. It matters little if there are choruses or not in the final scene. If it's only to have a crowd it's better to omit them.

Again we see Verdi rejecting a musical device (the chorus) not justified by the situation. Yet, in spite of his good intentions (he had promised Arrivabene that he would 'bury himself' in the problem), he wrote to Ricordi on June 22: 'Not wanting to hinder your affairs in the slightest, (. . .) do what you think best with this opera.'

Meanwhile the public, at performances in Florence, Rome and Genoa, was showing its dissatisfaction with the libretto and its grim conclusion. Verdi, aware of this from a number of reviews, laid the blame for the disastrous Genoa performance, at least, squarely on the singers. On April 14 1866 he wrote that he was too busy with the composition of *Don Carlos* (for the Paris Opéra) to revise the *Forza* dénouement. Since 1862 he had, however, been considering a French translation of *Forza*. This would require changes to accommodate the work to French taste, and the ending would be open for discussion. There was also question of a production in the original language at the Théâtre-Italien where, Verdi maintained, operas were treated as 'just so much merchandise'. (He later confided to his editor that the dénouement would have been something 'exceedingly disgusting' for that theatre.) Thus, while unwilling to revise the finale for Italian theatres, Verdi thought he would be unable to avoid changing the 'damned ending' in either of the proposed versions for Paris.

Negotiations for a translated *Forza* were tied to a commission for a new work for the Opéra, to be either a *Cleopatra*, a *Don Carlos*, or a *King Lear*. Once these terms were agreed, Verdi began considering the necessary alterations, but left the dénouement to be decided by the Opéra. The translators, Camille du Locle and Charles Nuitter, had already drafted alternatives for several scenes, including the finale. Some of these derived from Rivas's play, while others were of their own invention. Curiously, both their versions of the finale included, as in the play, Alvaro's suicide and the taunts of Carlos/Alfonso to the fatal duel. It would appear that they were striving to find an ending that the Parisians would find logical, without worrying whether they would recoil at so much carnage onstage.

Verdi arrived in Paris around the beginning of December, and very soon saw that it was unrealistic to try to revise and stage *Forza* in so little time. It was not only the amount of work to be done but also the nature of it that discouraged him. He had described his efforts in revising *Macbeth* on December 31, 1864, to Escudier:

> You cannot imagine how boring and difficult it is to work oneself up for something all over again, and to find a thread that has been broken for so many years. Doing it doesn't take long — but I detest *mosaics* in music.

A new contract, for *Don Carlos* alone, was announced to the press in December 1865. Thus, despite all the energy expended over more than three years, the projected *Force du destin* was never realized.

La Scala 1965/66: Piero Cappuccilli as Don Carlos (Teatro alla Scala: Archivio Fotografico)

Meanwhile the opera had established itself in the international repertory. Until 1865 the only further productions outside Italy had been repeat performances at St Petersburg and Madrid; thereafter it was performed in Vienna, North and South America, and London. But its reputation was hardly one of which Verdi could be especially proud. In a review of the Paris première of *Don Carlos* (1867), Eduard Hanslick held up the 1865 Vienna production of *Forza* (itself the object of unfavourable criticism) for comparison (*Leipziger Allgemeine Musikalische Zeitung*, November 13, 1867):

> We find Verdi's new style already prepared in the ponderous fourth act of *A Masked Ball*, and completely impressed upon that collection of musical accidents, which was served up in Vienna under the title *The Force of Destiny* . . . . The libretto of the new opera [i.e. *Don Carlos*] is considerably freer of palpable defects . . .

The critic of *The Musical Times* (July 1, 1867) pointedly put himself above the common public (which received the opera well) and wrote:

> It is idle to talk of a composer being crippled from the nature of his *libretto*. Verdi deliberately chooses revolting subjects, because it is only these that his unreal effects can be fitly wedded to . . . . It would be impossible, and indeed we have no desire, to follow in detail the musical illustrations of a story such as we usually find in the penny 'sensation' romances which pass for literature with romantic housemaids.

Such fundamental aversion to the plot could scarcely be overcome by mere retouching. The consensus of opinion must have convinced Verdi that some action was necessary.

In August 1868 Tito Ricordi proposed a new production at La Scala, Milan, for early 1869, with the assumption that there would be a new finale. Verdi, seeing the chance simultaneously to redeem the work and reestablish good relations with Italy's foremost opera house, agreed, on condition that he approve the cast and direct in person. He told Ricordi that he would 'adjust the catastrophe' when he could, adding that the opera would be 'retouched in many places' at the same time. To assist Verdi in the task, Tito offered the services of his son Giulio and of the poet Antonio Ghislanzoni. This time Verdi did not object to working with Ghislanzoni. That he had three years earlier may seem surprising; Ghislanzoni, a music critic and former singer, had, like Verdi, professed to being an enemy of the 'number opera', and had boasted that his own works contained 'poetry that rebels against any metre, verses that burst forth insubordinately like foam from champagne'. But this rebelliousness may have been precisely what put Verdi off at first. In 1866 Ghislanzoni had called *melodramma* 'the most complete, the most sublime expression of dramatic art, of which music represents a most eloquent, domineering, sometimes overbearing, accessory, yet always an accessory.' In his relations with composers he was sometimes positively dictatorial; when rejecting a request to provide a libretto for Alfredo Catalani he decreed: 'Liberty to the poet to make and dramatise the libretto as best it pleases him, liberty to the composer to accept it' — hardly the sort of language to induce Verdi to collaborate with him. Verdi had consistently chosen librettists whom he could bend to his will; perhaps just because he had been unable to produce a solution, he now agreed to this partnership.

The job did not prove easier than on earlier attempts. 'Oh, it's difficult to adjust its legs!' exclaimed Verdi to Giulio (November 12, 1868), as he again tried to repair this 'wobbly table'. An ending was slow in coming — dangerously slow, in view of the little time left before rehearsals were to begin. Many ideas were considered, some of them very different from that finally settled upon. We know of one of these from a letter to Giulio in which Verdi listed his objections to it:

> One sees too much the stage-trick [*ficella*] in bringing back the gipsies at the end; also there would be too much disturbance of the colouring [*colorito*] of these final scenes. A gipsy scene would distract, prolong, and chill the action, which is the worst of evils. It's useless; once this accursed subject is admitted, the two siblings must die. It's easy to find a way to kill Carlo, even offstage; but it's rather difficult to make Leonora die. It matters little if it's a duet, trio, or chorus: it's necessary only to pay attention to the scene.
>
> I wouldn't like to hear the second-act finale here. It's a ceremony, a consecration that cannot be repeated. In sum the poet should not have anything but the stage in view; he needn't bother himself about the music. For me even a recitative would be fine. If the poet finds a way to end logically and theatrically well, the music will necessarily come out well.

Ghislanzoni responded (via Ricordi):

> Verdi is perfectly correct when he says that a gipsy scene would chill the effect. In my idea, this scene would be just an *apparition* or rather a *passage*, so that at the fall of the curtain the stage would not be all encumbered with monks.
>
> It doesn't seem to me that the composer noticed that I *would make*

The two faces of Leonora: Josephine Barstow, ENO, 1983 (photos: John Garner)

Leonora be wounded backstage, and thus the agony of Carlo would be excluded. In any case, then, all that would be added to give prominence to the dénouement would be accessory, and thus would never be of use in relieving the effect of the catastrophe. In my opinion, it would already be a great gain to exclude the agonies of these two.

With the physical removal of the *agonizzanti* a major element of the new finale was now in place. It was not enough; on November 24 Verdi told Giulio to publicise the opera without naming him as the composer (a practice at the Paris Opéra he had long been tempted to imitate), and said that it would be given with changes only if they turned out well. 'Thus far nothing has been found.'

Three days later a solution had been found. Whether one believes it was Verdi who arrived at it depends in part on how one interprets the letter in which he first mentions it; the first page is lacking:

> . . . see Alvaro end so resigned? I have my great doubts about it which will perhaps augment or diminish in a calmer state of mind. In the meanwhile let Ghislanzoni judge, and if he doesn't like it, we'll look again.

Renata Tebaldi as Leonora at La Scala in the 1954/55 season (Teatro alla Scala: Archivio Fotografico)

Verdi's idea or not, he had strong reservations still. If, as Julian Budden suggests, the inspiration came from Verdi's veneration of Alessandro Manzoni and his masterwork, *I Promessi sposi* [*The Betrothed*] (Verdi had just recently met the author), his 'grave doubts' may have been about whether such a conclusion would be consistent with the tone of the rest of the opera. His doubts suggest also that the idea had not originated with him, and circumstances tend to indicate that the initiative for a Manzonian conclusion was provided by Ghislanzoni, who had simultaneously been turning Manzoni's novel into a libretto for Errico Petrella; the work had its première in Lecco on October 2, 1869.

A comparison of Manzoni's novel and Ghislanzoni's libretto of *I Promessi sposi* may give us an idea which version, if either, served as a model for Verdi's new dénouement. Ghislanzoni reordered and compressed Chapters 35 and 36 into two extremely economical scenes. In Chapter 35, Renzo, after cursing Don Rodrigo (the abductor of his betrothed, Lucia), is reprimanded by Padre Cristoforo and brought before the dying Rodrigo, whom he forgives. In the next chapter, he comes upon Lucia, relates these events to her, and brings Padre Cristoforo to free her from her rashly-sworn vow of chastity. Renzo bids farewell to Padre Cristoforo and asks where they shall next meet. *'Lassù, spero'* ('In Heaven above, I hope'), is his reply.

Ghislanzoni casts the conclusions of both operas as a duet followed by a trio. In *I Promessi sposi* Renzo finds Lucia (now in a procession of religious women) and, after learning of her vow, curses Rodrigo and his own hopeless situation (corresponding to Alvaro's *'Maledizione, maledizione!'*). Padre Cristoforo then enters with language reminiscent of the Padre Guardiano's *'Non imprecare, umiliati'* (i.e. Curse not, humble yourself) — Padre Cristoforo's words are *'L'uom che tu abbori — cui morte imprechi'* ('The man whom you

Nicolai Ghiaurov as Father Guardiano in the 1962 Covent Garden production (photo: Houston Rogers)

abhor — whom you curse as he dies') (the novel had not used this verb here). Petrella's opera ends with Rodrigo's death, Padre Cristoforo's gesture heavenward, and a reappearance of the procession of women; in the revision of *Forza* Leonora dies and is described as *'salita a Dio'* ('risen to God'). And, let us remember, Ghislanzoni had at one point wanted to end with a procession of gipsies — a scenic apparition akin to that of the religious women in *I Promessi sposi*. There are reasons why Ghislanzoni would not have hesitated at making use of a model: first, lack of time; second (despite his statements to the contrary) his proneness to fill his librettos with rather square poetry unless asked to do otherwise, as he was to be by Verdi in the case of *Aida*. If it already existed by the end of 1868, the libretto (or at least a plan) of *I Promessi sposi* would have offered a tempting model for the *Forza* finale, one easier to follow than the novel.

By mid-December the finale had been versified, and Verdi, now in Genoa, could report to Giulio that its composition was proceeding well. For more than a month Verdi continued to elicit textual changes from Ghislanzoni. First in importance was a text to replace the aria for Alvaro which in 1862 ended Act Three. As was his custom, Verdi himself suggested a text, to be cleaned up by the librettist:

I would also have desired at the end of the first duet between Carlo and Alvaro that Alvaro's resolution to become a monk be expressed more evidently. Something with action like, for example, throwing himself on his knees

Sii ringraziato a Dio	Thanks be to God
arme del guerriero lungi da me per sempre	hence from me forever the warrior's arms
M'allontano dal mondo e finirò in un chiostro etc.	remove me from the world and I'll end my days in a cloister etc.

45

Katherine Pring as Preziosilla and Terence Sharpe as Don Carlos at ENO (photo: Donald Southern)

In sum, something not fleeting, but quite clear and quite evident, from which the public can understand the rest of the drama and not be surprised at the appearance of Alvaro as a monk.

The need to clarify Alvaro's intentions was crucial now that his religious, rather than self-destructive, side was to prevail. In the 1862 aria, a life of religious retreat seemed to be Alvaro's second choice, if death were denied him. The aria in facts ends with him exclaiming *'Si voli a morte, e sia compita la sorte'* (i.e. Let me fly unto death, and let fate be accomplished). In Ghislanzoni's version, Alvaro's lines are resolute and unambiguous:

Or che mi resta? Pietoso Iddio,	What hope is left me? O God of mercy
Tu ispira, illumina il mio pensier . . .	Oh hear me, come to inspire me . . .
Al chiostro, all'eremo, ai santi altari,	A cloister, a hermitage, some holy altar
L'oblio, la pace chiegga il guerrier.	May bring me the peace my heart yearns to find.

The adjustments continued far into January. Whether from exasperation with how long they were taking, or from a genuine disinterest in the tone of the new ending, Verdi began to poke fun at its seriousness. Calling Ghislanzoni's poetry 'Christian verses', on January 11 he asked that two lines of text be changed, since he had already set his own earlier version to music. (The lines in question: 'Wherefore to avoid the bloody struggle / I tried everything', were now dangerously appropriate!) Similarly, on January 20 Verdi sent the recitative text where Carlos is wounded, explaining:

All this to retain some harmonies that were in the old piece. Show it to Ghislanzoni and ask if it can stay.

Norman Bailey as Don Carlos at the inn in the ENO production (photo: John Garner)

Rather than recompose this music (for which Ghislanzoni had supplied new words), Verdi retained that of the original version, retouching it ingeniously. He continued:

> Farther on in the trio when Alvaro becomes a good little boy [*buon figliuolo*] I would need a line for Leonora and the Guardiano.

Such humorous detachment from Alvaro's moment of conversion should caution us against attributing more to Verdi's motives than a desire for the best theatrical effect. On January 22 Verdi wrote that he would send Ricordi the final trio the next day, just as rehearsals were to begin. Almost to the last, however, he was reluctant to let the changes in the opera be announced.

Even if he could joke about it, Verdi still considered the final trio vital to the success of the opera. Critics, reporting the resounding triumph of the second première on February 27, bore him out for the most part. Pungolo, for instance:

> The fourth act, where the drama resumes its lugubrious development, and precipitates to the catastrophe, appears to us the most complete — in poetry, lyricism and musical drama. The music there speaks the tremendous and vivid language of passion.

Ghislanzoni's own perceptive résumé of the opera and its performance appeared on March 7. The article was signed: Ghislanzoni could safely do this since his collaboration with Verdi was not generally known. He saw the play's 'Spanish exaggeration', 'chivalric pride', and 'monastic fanaticism' as just those features which attracted Verdi to it. Rivas's drama was 'immoderately grim for the Italian stage', but it did provide 'not a few situations very suitable for music, and passions, characters and tableaux that are very effective in the theatre.'

Ghislanzoni continued with an insider's account:

> It was necessary to reflect a lot before coming to a less murderous solution that did not contradict the title of the opera, or rather the Spanish poet's predominating idea. *Fatality* required that Don Alvaro exterminate the entire Vargas family . . . It was a matter then of letting fate fulfil its tremendous decree, and of sparing the spectators the sight of so many victims.

We should take him at his word — Verdi had been saying as much since 1863. (It is also not impossible that the composer suggested some of what went into Ghislanzoni's review.) Ghislanzoni adds that:

> before deciding for the trio, he [Verdi] weighed all the combinations that were proposed to him, discussed them at length, and we believe that he chose for the best.

Even in print Ghislanzoni says, in effect, that the new finale (or at least the form it would take) was not of Verdi's invention; yet he lauds his 'almost infallible dramatic intuition', with which 'he is accustomed to assimilating the conceits of the poet, coordinating and directing them'. The experience of working with a master of Verdi's stature seems to have made Ghislanzoni more humble than was his wont.

*

One is hard pressed to state a preference for either of the two endings. The tortured route by which Verdi came to the new finale, and his doubts even after it was chosen, do not give it an authority that would consign the original to the scrap-heap. Both are to some extent successful in following up themes from earlier in the opera, but in neither do dramatic and musical strengths go hand in hand.

In the 1862 ending Alvaro and the monks carry the drama to a conclusion which follows inevitably from their previous appearances. The credit for this goes mainly to Rivas, but Verdi seconds the playwright with music that matches the stark intensity of the scene. Alvaro, described shortly before by Melitone as a demon incarnate, hurls himself into Hell, fulfilling the death-wish he made at the end of the 1862 Act Three. The monk's powerful *'Maledizione'* chorus at the end of Act Two is of a weight that assures the spectator that the hermit's grotto *will* be violated, and their *'Miserere'* in the finale effectively balances the earlier number. The revised final scene connects ideas over longer distances and by subtler means. Alvaro's repulsion of Leonora recalls her hesitations in the opening elopement scene. His despair when, having just killed Carlos, he recognises Leonora, reminds one of his state of mind at the *beginning* of Act Three. So does his music — Verdi uses the mournful clarinet sounds that had characterised No. 16. The presence of the Padre Guardiano is also more effective than a swarm of monks in linking the theme of spiritual redemption to Alvaro.

Momentum is crucial to both finales — in the first it builds inexorably towards a precipitous conclusion, while in the second it is intentionally prevented from developing. In 1862, there is a steady crescendo produced by worsening weather, shorter text lines and an increase in the number of characters on stage. The *pianissimo* at the end is felt more as a reverberation of the preceding horror and fury than as a real sense of repose. In 1869, Verdi

Rosa Ponselle as Leonora in disguise at the Met. in 1918 (photo: Ida Cook Collection)

Giuseppe Fancelli as Don Alvaro

restrains the pace in several ways. The first step was the removal of the duel and of Leonora's onstage stabbing. Nature is made to cooperate, too — the original storm at *'Pace, pace'* (No. 33) becomes simply 'nightfall'. Finally, the music retained from the 1862 finale is rhythmically stretched and shorn of some of its dialogue, so that it no longer has the power to propel a cabaletta-like outburst.

The problems in the new version begin with the entrance of the Padre Guardiano. Up to that point Verdi had done a masterful job of joining new music to old. Taken by itself, the final trio is impressive; one perceives the care with which it was constructed. But the splice is too evident. A lyrical period follows too incongruously after what has just taken place, both musically and dramatically. Verdi had handled a similar situation in *I Lombardi* (*The Lombards*, 1843) far more naturally; in the Act Three finale, the hermit's admonishments interrupt the *cantabile* of Giselda's curses and there is recitative for some time before a lyrical melody can assert itself. Also troubling are the dramatic contradictions of the piece. After the Padre Guardiano's speech, Leonora promises Alvaro God's forgiveness, which he accepts. Thereupon she sings a stanza beginning *'Lieta poss'io precederti'* ('Gladly I go to wait for you'), which derives from a line in the earlier libretto *'Ci rivedremo in ciel'* ('We'll meet again in Heaven'). There the idea had been a cliché (and not a very apt one, since Alvaro's salvation had been very much in doubt), but now it sets the tone for the opera's conclusion. Alvaro's subsequent complaint:

Tu mi condanni a vivere	Am I condemned to linger on . . .
E m'abbandoni intanto!	Alone on earth you leave me!
Il reo, il reo soltanto	The guilty one alone lives on unpunished
Dunque impunito andrà!	Though I alone transgressed.

is hard to reconcile with Leonora's words, and with his redemption just previously, which an exalted harmonic shift made a real turning point. Before, Alvaro had always been steadfast (as in the two duets with Carlos) until he gave way to his emotions, when he did so utterly. If we are to believe this new text, we must conclude that Alvaro has quickly lapsed from faith in his redemption.

A more reasonable conclusion to draw would be that Verdi simply felt uncomfortable with such orthodox piety, and could not bring off a finale espousing it (no matter how highly he regarded Manzoni). Just at this time in *Don Carlos* he expressed his firm belief that this world offers no real solace, even in a life of religious retreat. The point is also driven home again and again in this opera. The difference between the two versions boils down to the fact that by 1869 he was capable of much subtler means of expressing this idea than his protagonist's leap from a cliff. But in such a bold Spanish epic a subtle ending was perhaps not the most appropriate one.

For Verdi the new ending was a definitive revision, meant to put the work in the good graces of public and critics alike, once and for all. Yet, though he had agonized over the problem for six years, the result still gives the impression of a job done in haste, without the full force of his enthusiasm behind it. The genesis of the new finale was a remarkably public process, in which the opinions of friends, colleagues, critics, and audiences played important parts. While Verdi bristled at the criticisms of individual journalists, it can hardly be denied that these made a cumulative impression on him, and most of all when they reported the reaction of the public; for, had audiences not been genuinely dissatisfied with the finale, Verdi would surely have left it alone.

Design by Franco Lolli for Act Two scene one for the 1953 Maggio Musicale, Florence
Design by Giovanni Grandi for Act Three scene three at La Scala in 1946

Design by Edoardo Marchioro for Act Four scene two at La Scala in 1927
Design by Orlando di Collalto for Act Four scene two at the Verona Arena in 1959

53

Thematic Guide

Many of the themes from the opera have been identified in the articles by numbers in square brackets, which refer to the themes set out on these pages. The themes are also identified by the numbers in square brackets at the corresponding points in the libretto, so that the words can be related to the musical themes.

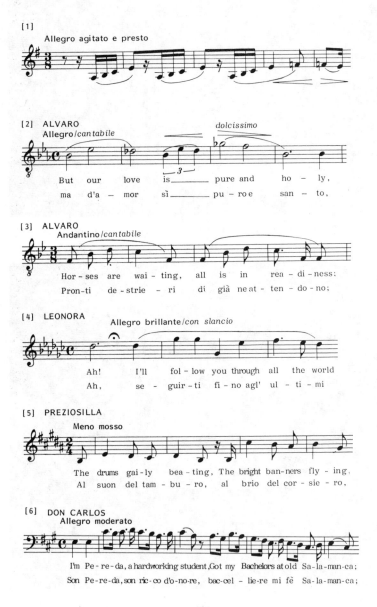

[1] Allegro agitato e presto

[2] ALVARO
Allegro/cantabile
dolcissimo

But our love is_____ pure and ho — ly,
ma d'a — mor sì_____ pu — ro e san — to,

[3] ALVARO
Andantino/cantabile

Hor — ses are wai — ting, all is in rea — di — ness;
Pron — ti de — strie — ri di già ne at — ten — do — no;

[4] LEONORA
Allegro brillante/con slancio

Ah! I'll fol — low you through all the world
Ah, se — guir — ti fi — no agl' ul — ti — mi

[5] PREZIOSILLA
Meno mosso

The drums gai — ly bea — ting, The bright ban — ners fly — ing.
Al suon del tam — bu — ro, al brio del cor — sie — ro,

[6] DON CARLOS
Allegro moderato

I'm Pe — re — da, a hardworking student,Got my Bachelors at old Sa — la — man — ca;
Son Pe — re — da, son ric — co d'o — no — re, bac — cel — lie — re mi fè Sa — la — man — ca;

[7] LEONORA
Allegro assai moderato/*sotto voce come lamento*

Vir – gin, Vir – gin look down and com – fort me,
Ma – dre, Ma – dre, pie-to – sa Ver – gi –ne,

[8] LEONORA
Allegro agitato

I'm un – happy, de-ser-ted, accur – sed, And re-jec-ted by earth and by Hea-ven,
In-fe – li-ce, de-lu-sa, re-jet – ta, dal-la ter-ra e dal ciel ma-le-det – ta,

[9] LEONORA
Andante mosso

How my sor-row has been lightened since I trod this ho –ly ground;
Più tran-quil-la l'al-ma sen-to dac-chè pre-mo que-sta ter – ra;

[10]

LEONORA
Ah my sor-row has been lightened,
Più tran-quil-la l'al – ma sen-to,

GUARDIANO
Who can read the fu – ture, or be cer – tain of his heart?
clouded
Nel fu-tu – ro chi può leggere, chi immu-ta – bil far vi il cor?

[11] GUARDIANO
Poco più mosso

Praise be to Hea – ven for this great mer – cy,
A te sia glo – ria, o Dio cle – men – te,

[12] GUARDIANO
Moderato/*cantabile*

At mor-ning light you'll seek that cave, the path lies clear be – fore you;
Sull' al-ba il pie-de all' e – re-mo so – lin-ga vol-ge-re – te;

[13] LEONORA
Più mosso

O Fa – ther I thank Thee, Thou smil'st on this poor sin — ner!
Tua gra – zia, o Di – o, sor-ri-de al-la re – jet – ta!

55

[14] GUARDIANO
Allegro assai moderato

The ho - ly cave to him shall be open-ed. You know the place?
Il san - to spe-co noi le schiu - dia-mo. V'è no-to il lo - co?

[15] CHORUS
Adagio/sotto voce

The ble - ssed Vir - gin pray for thee be - neath her man - tle
La Ver - gi - ne de - gli an - ge - li vi co - pra del suo

[16] ALVARO
Andante sostenuto

High in the realms of Pa - ra - dise
Oh, tu che in se - no agl' an - ge - li

[17] ALVARO
Andante sostenuto

In death's so - lemn mo - ment oh grant me one fa - vour
So - len - ne in quest' o - ra giu - rar - mi do - ve - te

[18] CARLOS
Andante sostenuto/cantabile

Ah, fa-tal my-st'ry, hiding my fu-ture, Get you behind me, in vain you tempt me;
Ur-na fa-ta-le del mio de-sti-no, va, t'al-lon-ta-na, mi ten - ti in-va - no;

[19] ALVARO
Allegro mosso

Dis-loy-al! You have bro-ken a vow that was sa - cred.
Sle - a - le! Il se - gre - to fu dun-que vio - la - to?

[20] ALVARO
Andantino/cantabile

No, we'll ful-fil that sa-cred vow By which our hearts were pligh - ted!
No, d'un i-me-ne il vin-co-lo strin-ga fra noi la spe - me;

56

[21] MELITONE
Allegro moderato

I left my cloister to me-dicate the wounded men-dicate their What find I?
and souls.

Ven-ni di Spa-gna a me-di-car fe - ri - te, ed al-me a mendi-car. Che ve - do?

[22] PREZIOSILLA
Allegro vivo

Rata – plan, rata-plan, on to glo - ry drums are beating and bugles re - ply,

Rata – plan, rata-plan, del-la glo - ria pel sol-da-to ri-tempra l'ar-dor,

[23] V'Cellos

[24] GUARDIANO   MELITONE
Andante mosso

The world and _ life's de - lu - sions,   The world and its de - lu-sions,

Del mon - do i di-sin - gan-ni,   Sa-ran-noi di-sin - gan-ni,

[25] CARLOS
Sostenuto

By blood a – lone can we be saved

Col san – gue sol can - cel - la-si

[26] ALVARO
Andante/cantabile, con espress.

All your fie - ry threats of ven - geance

Le mi - nac-cie,i fie-ri ac - cen - ti

[27] LEONORA
Andante

Fa – ther, Fa – ther, Fa-ther in Heaven, gra-nt me peace of mind!

Pa - ce, pa – ce, pa-ce mio Di-o, pa-ce,mio Di - o!

[28] GUARDIANO
Andante sostenuto

Do not bla – spheme but kneel and pray

Non im-pre - ca - re,u-mi - lia - ti.

57

Giuseppe di Stefano as Alvaro at La Scala in 1956/57 (Teatrale alla Scala: Archivio Fotografico)

Antonietta Stella as Leonora at La Scala in 1956/7 (Teatro alla Scala: Archivio Fotografico)

The Force of Destiny
La Forza del Destino

Opera in Four Acts
Music by Giuseppe Verdi
Libretto by Francesco Maria Piave
(with additions by Antonio Ghislanzoni)
after the play, *Don Alvaro, o La Fuerza del sino*,
by Angel de Saavedra, Duke of Rivas,
with a scene added from Schiller's *Wallensteins Lager*
translated by Andrea Maffei

English translation by Andrew Porter

The first version of *The Force of Destiny* was first given at the Bolshoi Theatre, St Petersburg, on November 10, 1862. This was performed in New York on February 24, 1865 and in London at Her Majesty's on June 22, 1867.

The second version was first performed at La Scala, Milan, on February 27, 1869.

CHARACTERS

The Marquis of Calatrava (Il Marchese di Calatrava)	*bass*
Donna Leonora *his daughter*	*soprano*
Don Carlos de Vargas *his son* (Don Carlo di Vargas)	*baritone*
Don Alvaro	*tenor*
Preziosilla *a young gipsy girl*	*mezzo-soprano*
Father Guardiano ⎫ *Franciscans* (Il Padre Guardiano)	*bass*
Melitone ⎭ (Fra Melitone)	*baritone*
Curra *Leonora's maid*	*mezzo-soprano*
The Alcalde (Alcade)	*bass*
Trabuco *muleteer, then pedlar* (Maestro Trabuco)	*tenor*
A Spanish military surgeon	*tenor*

Muleteers — Spanish and Italian peasants — Spanish and Italian soldiers of various ranks — orderlies — Italian recruits — monks — peasant girls and vivandières

Ballet Peasants — soldiers — vivandières

Mimes Host — hostess — inn-servants — muleteers — soldiers — drummers — buglers — peasants — children — a tumbler — various sutlers

The action takes place in Spain and Italy.
Epoch: towards the middle of the eighteenth century.

Editor's Note

The Italian title Padre Guardiano ought literally to be translated as Father Guardian. An unfortunate custom has developed of mixing the two languages in this case.

English translations usually prefer the names of characters according to the place where the action is set rather than the language of the original libretto. Hence 'Don Carlo' here becomes 'Don Carlos' (as in Rivas), and the Italian 'Alcade' becomes the Spanish 'Alcalde'.

Act One

Seville

Scene One. *A hall hung with damask and family portraits and coats of arms in 18th-century style, although all is shabby. Two windows face the audience; through the one that is open, giving onto a balcony, clear moonlight can be seen above the trees. A large wardrobe between the windows contains dresses, linen, etc.. Doors on the right, one to the main stairway, the other to Curra's room; on the left, the nearer one leads to Leonora's room, the farther to that of the Marquis. In mid-stage, a little to the left, a little table covered with damask; on it a guitar and flower-vases, and two lighted silver candlesticks with shades, the only source of light in the room. A large chair near the table, between the two doors: right a piece of furniture with a clock; to the left another piece of furniture over which hangs a full-length portrait of the Marquis. The room has an outside balcony. / No. 1 Introduction and Scena*

MARQUIS
(embracing Leonora affectionately)

Goodnight, Leonora, goodnight, my daughter.	Buona notte, mia figlia . . . Addio diletta.
Why is this window open still? . . .	Aperto ancora è quel veron! . . .

(He goes to close it.)

LEONORA

(My anguish!)	(Oh! angoscia!)

MARQUIS
(turning to her)

Have you nothing to say? So sad and silent?	Nulla dice il tuo amor? . . . Perchè sì triste?

LEONORA

Father . . . My lord . . .	Padre . . . Signor . . .

MARQUIS

The country air will cure you, Calm your unhappy spirits . . . And you'll forget that worthless foreign stranger . . . Let your father take care of your future life. Will you not trust me, your father who loves you dearly?	La pura aura de' campi Pace al tuo cor donava . . . Fuggisti lo straniero di te indegno . . . A me lascia la cura Dell'avvenir. Nel padre tuo confida Che t'ama tanto.

LEONORA

Oh father!	Ah padre!

MARQUIS

What's this, what ails you? No tears now.	Ebben, che t'ange? Non pianger . . .

LEONORA

(I'm remorseful!)	(Oh rimorso!)

MARQUIS

I'll leave you.	Ti lascio.

LEONORA
(throwing herself with great emotion into his arms)

My dearest father!	Ah padre mio!

MARQUIS

May Heaven protect and bless you. Good night now!	Ti benedica il cielo . . . Addio!

LEONORA

Good night now.	Addio!

(The Marquis takes his candle and goes off to his room.)

Scene Two. *Curra sees the Marquis to the door and returns to Leonora who throws herself into the chair and gives way to her grief.* / *No. 2 Recitative and Romanza*

CURRA

I thought that he would stay here till the morning!

Temea restasse qui fino a domani!

I'll open the window again . . . and now get ready.

Si riapra il veron . . . tutto s'appronti.

(She does so.)

We're leaving.

E andiamo.

(She takes a travelling bag from the wardrobe and starts packing linen and clothes.)

LEONORA

How can my loving father so sternly
Oppose those joys I long for?
No, no, I cannot yet decide.

E si amoroso padre avverso
Fia tanto a' voti miei?
No, no, decidermi non so.

CURRA
(packing quickly)

What nonsense!

Che dite?

LEONORA

Every word he spoke entered my heart
Like a dagger thrust . . . If he'd stayed longer
I would have told him all.

Quegli accenti nel cor come pugnali
Scendevanmi . . . Se ancor restava, appreso
Il ver gli avrei . . .

CURRA
(She stops packing.)

And then tomorrow Don Alvaro
Would lie in a pool of blood,
Or in Seville in a dungeon, or die
Upon the scaffold . . .

Domani allor nel sangue
Suo saria Don Alvaro,
Od a Siviglia prigioniero, e forse
Al patibol poi . . .

LEONORA

Silence!

Taci.

CURRA

And this he'd suffer
Because he loved a lady who didn't love him.

E tutto questo
Perch'egli volle armar chi non l'amava.

LEONORA

Ah! I not love him? You know well I love him.
Country, and kindred, father,
For him I am deserting!
My sorrow! I am doomed to endless sorrow!

Io non amarlo? . . . Tu ben sai s'io l'ami . . .
Patria, famiglia, padre
Per lui non abbandono?
Ahi, troppo! . . . troppo sventurata sono!

Now I must leave my native land,
New stars will shine above me,
For destiny conspires, alas,
To part me from those who love me . . .

Me pellegrina ed orfana
Lungi dal patrio nido
Un fato inesorabile
Sospinge a stranio lido . . .

Thousands of sad imaginings
Fill all my soul with horror,
And cares oppress the heart of one
Whom fate condemns to endless sorrow . . .

Colmo di tristi immagini,
Da' suoi rimorsi affranto
È il cor di questa misera
Dannato a eterno pianto . . .

(with the deepest grief)

I leave, alas, alas, in tears I leave,
My native country! I leave you!
Alas, alas, before me I see
Only endless sorrow! I leave you!

Ti lascio, ahimè, con lacrime,
Dolce mia terra! Addio!
Ahimè, non avrà termine
Sì gran dolore! . . . Addio!

O Spain, in tears I leave you.
I leave my beloved country.
Alas, I see no destiny
But endless sorrow! I leave you!

Ti lascio, ahimè, con lacrime,
Dolce mia terra! Addio!
Ahimè, non avrà termine
Sì gran dolore! . . . Addio!

CURRA

Please help me, señorita . . .   M'aiuti, signorina . . .
We'll soon be done.   Più presto andrem . . .

LEONORA

What if he failed me?   S'ei non venisse?
(She looks at the clock.)
It's late now.   È tardi!
(happily)
Surely midnight has sounded!   Mezzanotte è suonata!
(joyously)
Ah no, he will not come!   Ah no, più non verrà! . . .

CURRA

Galloping horses!   Quale rumore!
They're under the window . . .   Calpestio di cavalli . . .

LEONORA
(She runs to the window.)

Alvaro!   E desso! . . .

CURRA

Oh, I was certain   Era impossibil
He would not fail us!   Ch'ei non venisse!

LEONORA

Oh Heavens!   Oh Dio!

CURRA

Banish your fear!   Bando al timore!

Scene Three. *Don Alvaro without a cloak, but wearing a wide-sleeved tunic, a Majo's doublet and knitted cap, and booted and spurred, enters through the open window and throws himself into Leonora's arms.*

ALVARO

Mine for ever, my beloved,   Ah! per sempre, o mio bell'angiol,
Heaven rewards the love we plighted!   Ne congiunge il cielo adesso!
Now at last we are united,   L'universo in questo amplesso
Now for ever you are mine.   Io mi veggo giubilar.

LEONORA

Don Alvaro!   Don Alvaro!

ALVARO

Ah, what troubles you?   Ciel, che t'agita?

LEONORA

Day approaches . . .   Presso è il giorno . . .

ALVARO

By a thousand   Da lung'ora
Strange adventures, fate and chance   Mille inciampi tua dimora
Conspired to keep me from your side;   M'han vietato penetrar;
But our love is pure and holy,   [2] Ma d'amor si puro e santo
Love like ours is all-victorious.   Nulla opporsi può all'incanto,
God himself has blessed our love,   E Dio stesso il nostro palpito
And our sorrow turns to joy.   In letizia tramutò.
(to Curra)
Throw the bags down from the window!   Quelle vesti dal verone
Hurry!   Getta . . .

LEONORA
(to Curra)

One moment.   Arresta.

ALVARO
(to Curra)

No, no . . .   No, no . . .
(to Leonora)
Follow me,   Seguimi.
Leave your prison cell behind you.   Lascia omai la tua prigione . . .

LEONORA

Ah! How can I leave my home?   Ciel! risolvermi non so.
No, I cannot leave my home.   No, risolvermi non so.

ALVARO

Horses are waiting, all is in readiness;   [3] Pronti destrieri di già ne attendono;
There at the altar a priest expects us . . .   Un sacerdote ne aspetta all'ara . . .
Come, my beloved, welcome your freedom,   Vieni, d'amore in sen ripara
For God in Heaven blesses our love!   Che Dio dal cielo benedirà!

And when the sunlight, God of the Incas,   E quando il sole, nume dell'India,
Father and founder of my royal lineage,   Di mia regale stirpe signore,
Shines on the world with his glorious pure   Il mondo inondi del suo splendore,
  ray,
O my beloved, we shall be wed.   Sposi, o diletta, ne troverà.

LEONORA

The hour is late . . .   È tarda l'ora . . .

ALVARO
(to Curra)

And we are ready!   Su via, t'affrettta.

LEONORA
(to Curra)

But wait a moment . . .   Ancor sospendi . . .

ALVARO

Leonora!   Eleonora!

LEONORA

Tomorrow . . .   Diman . . .

ALVARO

What madness!   Chi parli?

LEONORA

Oh, do not press me!   Ten prego, aspetta!

ALVARO
(very agitated)

Tomorrow!   Diman!

LEONORA

Tomorrow I shall escape.   Dimani si partirà.
Just one day longer to see my father,   Anco una volta il padre mio,
Ah, my poor father, how can I leave him;   Povero padre, veder desio;
You won't refuse me, I'm sure, I'm sure?   E tu contento, gli è ver, ne sei?
Because you love me . . .   Sì, perchè m'ami . . .
(embarrassed)
You won't refuse me . . .   nè opporti dei . . .
You know I love you . . . I love you dearly!   Anch'io, tu il sai . . . t'amo io tanto!
I love you dearly and I'm so happy!   Ne son felice! . . . oh cielo, quanto!
(weeping)
Bursting with joy, my heart! I'll stay   Gonfio di gioia ho il cor! Restiamo . . .
  here . . .

64

Yes, my Alvaro, I love you! . . . I love you! . . .	Sì, Don Alvaro, io t'amo! . . . io t'amo! . . .

(*overcome*)

ALVARO

Bursting with joy your heart . . . and tears of grief!	Gonfio hai di gioia il core . . . lagrimi!
Fearful and trembling, your hands as cold as ice!	Come un sepolcro tua mano è gelida! . . .
I understand you plainly, my lady.	Tutto comprendo . . . tutto, signora . . . signora . . .

LEONORA

Alvaro! Alvaro!	Alvaro! . . . Alvaro! . . .

ALVARO

Leonora!	Eleonora! . . .

(*a long pause*)

But I alone must suffer . . . God forbid it	Io sol saprò soffrire . . . Tolga Iddio
If you decide to follow me through weakness . . .	Che i passi miei per debolezza segua . . .
I now release you. For the marriage altar	Sciolgo i tuoi giuri . . . Le nuziali tede
Would be a place of doom whose vows destroy us	Sarebbero per noi segnal di morte . . .
If you don't love as I do . . . If repentant . . .	Se tu, com'io, non m'ami . . . se pentita . . .

LEONORA
(*interrupting*)

Ah no, I'm yours, I am yours alone for ever.	Son tua, son tua col core e colla vita.

Ah! I'll follow you through all the world	[4]	Ah, seguirti fino agli ultimi
If you are near to guide me;		Confini della terra;
I'll gladly brave a thousand deaths		Con te sfidar impavida
If you remain beside me,		Di rio destin la guerra,
For you are all in all to me,		Mi fia perenne gaudio
My only source of joy.		D'eterna voluttà.
I love you with a love		Ti seguo . . . Andiam, dividerci
That Fate never can destroy.		Il fato non potrà.

ALVARO

Leonora, life and light to me,	Sospiro, luce ed anima
Recall that vow I swore you:	Di questo cor che t'ama;
My heart, my hand, my very soul	Finchè mi batta un palpito
I gladly lay before you,	Far paga ogni tua brama
For you are all in all to me,	Il solo ed immutabile
My only source of joy.	Desio per me sarà.
I love you with a love that Fate	Mi segui . . . Andiam, dividerci
Never can destroy.	Il mondo non potrà.

(*They move toward the window, when suddenly doors are heard being opened and closed.*)

LEONORA

What is that noise?	Quale rumor!

CURRA
(*listening*)

There's someone on the staircase!	Ascendono le scale!

ALVARO

Away . . .	Partiam . . .

No. 4 Scena. Finale One

LEONORA

Too late now!	È tardi.

ALVARO

Be calm
Whatever happens.

Allor di calma
È d'uopo.

CURRA

Holy Virgin!

Vergin Santa!

LEONORA
(to Alvaro, pointing to her room)

Go into hiding!

Colà t'ascondi ...

ALVARO
(He pulls out a pistol.)

No, I'll stay here to defend you.

No. Degg'io difenderti.

LEONORA

But why that pistol ... You would never
fire
On my father?

Ripon quell'arma ... control al genitore
Vorresti? ...

ALVARO

No, against myself first ...

No, contro me stesso ...

(He replaces the pistol.)

LEONORA

Alvaro!

Orrore! ...

Scene Four. *After repeated blows the door is burst open, and the Marquis enters, furious, brandishing a sword, and followed by two footmen with lights.*

MARQUIS

Infamous wretch! And shameful daughter!

Vil seduttor! ... infame figlia!

LEONORA
(throwing herself at his feet)

O father, hear me ...

No, padre mio ...

MARQUIS
(repulsing her)

My child no longer ...

Io più nol sono ...

ALVARO
(to the Marquis)

Alone, I am guilty.
(indicating his sword and breast)
So kill me, take your revenge on me ...

Il solo colpevole son io.

Ferite, vendicatevi ...

MARQUIS
(to Alvaro)

No, for your vile conduct
Proves you of low-born lineage — I would
disdain to touch you!

No, la condotta vostra
Da troppo abbietta origine uscito vi
dimostra.

ALVARO
(indignantly)

Senor Marchese! ...

Signor Marchese! ...

MARQUIS
(to Leonora)

Stand away!
(to the footmen)
Arrest that fellow.

Scostati.

S'arresti l'empio.

ALVARO
(again drawing his pistol)

Dare   Guai

To touch me at your peril ...   Se alcun di voi si move ...

LEONORA
(running to him)

Alvaro, Alvaro, no!   Alvaro, o ciel, che fai!

ALVARO
(to the Marquis)

Only to you I'll yield ...   Cedo a voi sol, ferite ...

MARQUIS

You'd die by my hand!   Morir per mano mia!
Ah no, the common hangman will take   Per mano del carnefice tal vita spenta fia.
  your life tommorow!

ALVARO

My Lord of Calatrava! Pure as an angel is   Signor di Calatrava! ... Pura siccome gli
  your child,   angeli
She is pure, I swear it; I alone am guilty.   E vostra figlia, il giuro; reo son io solo. Il
                                               dubbio
In proof of your daughter's stainless virtue, Che l'ardir mio qui desta, si tolga colla vita.
Here is my pistol ...   Eccomi inerme ...

(He flings down the pistol. As it hits the ground, it goes off, mortally wounding the Marquis.)

MARQUIS

I'm dying!   Io muoio!

ALVARO
(in desperation)

Fatal misfortune!   Arma funesta!

LEONORA
(running to her father)

God help me!   Aita!

MARQUIS
(to Leonora)

Out of my sight ... The sight of you defiles Lungi da me ... Contamina tua vista la
  my dying moments.   mia morte.

LEONORA

Father!   Padre! ...

MARQUIS

Dying, I curse you!   Ti maledico.

(He falls back into the arms of the footmen.)

LEONORA
(in despair)

Heaven, have mercy!   Cielo, pietade!

ALVARO

Have mercy!   Oh sorte!

(The servants carry the Marquis to his apartments while Alvaro draws Leonora, fainting, to the balcony.)

The curtain falls.

Act Two

The village of Hornachuelos and Neighbourhood.

Scene One. *Large kitchen on the ground floor of an inn: To the left is the main door to the road, at the back a window and large dresser stacked with plates, etc.. To the right, a large fireplace with saucepans, etc.; downstage a staircase up to a door. A large table to one side is set for supper and above it burns a lamp; the landlord and his wife (non-speaking characters) are busy preparing supper. The Alcalde sits near the fire, a student by the table. Prominent among some muleteers is Trabuco, leaning on his saddle. Two peasants dance with their girls, a muleteer with a servant; Seguidilla — three couples. Another table has glasses, bottles, flasks and brandy keg: muleteers, peasants with their girls, families etc.. Later, Leonora in male attire. / No. 5 Danced Chorus (Seguidilla)*

CORUS

Holà, holà, holà!
Be welcome muleteer,
There's no more work today.
Holà, holà, holà!
Good wine awaits you here,
The mules have had their hay.

Holà, holà, holà!
Ben giungi, o mulattier,
La notte a riposar.
Holà, holà, holà!
Qui devi col bicchier
Le forze ritemprar!

Scena / The hostess places a large soup tureen on the table.

ALCALDE
(seating himself at the table)

And now to table ...

La cena è pronta ...

ALL
(taking seats at the table)

To table.

A cena.

STUDENT
(aside)

(I seek in vain my sister and her seducer ...
Curse them both!)

(Ricerco in van la suora e il seduttore ...
Perfidi!)

ALL
(to Alcalde)

Say the grace for us, Alcalde.

Voi la mensa benedite.

ALCALDE

Our student here can say it.

Può farlo il licenziato.

STUDENT

I am honoured:
In nomine Patris, et Filii, et Spiritus Sancti.

Di buon grado.
In nomine Patris, et Filii, et Spiritus Sancti.

ALL
(sitting down)

Amen.

Amen.

LEONORA
(She peeps timidly round the stairway door which she keeps half-closed.)

(I see him! There's my brother!)

(Che vedo! ... mio fratello! ...)

(She withdraws. The hostess, having served the rice, sits at the table with them; she serves another dish in due course. Trabuco, always aloof, leans on his saddle. One couple continue to dance while the others eat.)

ALCALDE
(tasting the soup)

Like it?

Buono.

STUDENT
(*tasting*)

It's delicious.   Eccellente.

ALL

Seems to murmur: 'Eat me up!'   Par che dica mangiami.

STUDENT
(*to the Hostess*)

Tu das epulis accumbere Divum.   *Tu das epulis accumbere Divum.*

ALCALDE

She's no good at Latin, but her cooking's   Non sa il latino, ma cucina bene.
  splendid.

STUDENT

Here's to the hostess!   Viva l'Ostessa!

ALL

Our hostess!   Evviva!

STUDENT

Trabuco does not   Non vien Mastro
Join us?   Trabuco?

TRABUCO

Today is Friday.   È venerdi.

STUDENT

You're fasting?   Digiuna?

TRABUCO

Precisely.   Appunto.

STUDENT

And where is that young person who was   E quella personcina con lei giunta? . . .
  with you?

Scene Two. *Enter Preziosilla, dancing. / No. 7 Recitative and Canzone*

PREZIOSILLA

Long live the army!   Viva la guerra!

ALL

Preziosilla! . . . Welcome!   Preziosilla! . . . Brava!
Welcome!   Brava!

STUDENT AND ALCALDE

Come sit by me . . .   Qui, presso a me . . .

ALL

Come sit by me . . .   Qui, presso a me . . .
You know the future, say what's in store.   Tu la ventura dirne potrai.

PREZIOSILLA

Who wants to make his fortune?   Chi brama far fortuna.

ALL

We one and all.   Tutti il vogliam.

PREZIOSILLA

Then join the army marching   Corrette allor soldati
To Italy, where Italians are bravely   In Italia, dov'è rotta la guerra
Fighting the enemy.*   Contro ai nemici . . .

---

* Like other references, the 1862 libretto has 'Tedesco' ('German') for enemy.

Death	Morte
To the enemy!	Ai nemici.

PREZIOSILLA

The scourge of all Italians,	Flagel d'Italia eterno
Blight on Italian soil.	E de' figliuoli suoi.

ALL

We'll go to war.	Tutti v'andrem.

PREZIOSILLA

And you will find me there.	Ed io sarò con voi.

The drums gaily beating,	[5] Al suon del tamburo,
The bright banners flying,	Al brio del corsiero,
The bugles in greeting	Al nugolo azzurro
As guns give reply;	Del bronzo guerriero,
The foemen retreating	Dei campi al susurro
Rejoice every eye!	S'esalta il pensiero!
Oh, war is exciting,	È bella la guerra!
Yes, war is exciting!	È bella la guerra!
Hurrah for the army! Evviva!	Evviva la guerra! Evviva!

ALL

Yes, war is exciting,	È bella la guerra!
Hurrah for the army! Evviva!	Evviva la guerra! Evviva!

PREZIOSILLA

The faint-hearted coward	E sol obliato
Will die unlamented;	Da vile chi muore;
The brave-hearted soldier	Al bravo soldato,
Delights in the war,	Al vero valore,
For glory awaits him	È premio serbato
And fame evermore!	Di gloria, d'onore!
Oh, war is exciting,	È bella la guerra!
Yes, war is exciting!	È bella la guerra!
Hurrah for the army! Evviva!	Evviva la guerra! Evviva!

ALL

Yes, war is exciting!	È bella la guerra!
Hurrah for the army! Evviva!	Evviva la guerra! Evviva!

PREZIOSILLA
(*turning from person to person*)

If you come to join us,	Se vieni, fratello,
You'll soon be a corporal;	Sarai caporale;
And you'll be a colonel;	E tu colonnello,
And you'll be a general . . .	E tu generale . . .
And when the battle's over	Il dio furfantello
Then new joys await you,	Dall'arco immortale
For love will reward	Farà di cappello
Every brave soldier-boy . . .	Al bravo uffiziale.
Oh, war is exciting,	È bella la guerra!
Yes, war is exciting!	È bella la guerra!
Hurrah for the army! Evviva!	Evviva la guerra! Evviva!

ALL

Hurrah for the army! Evviva!	Evviva la guerra! Evviva!

STUDENT
(*offering his hand to be read*)

Tell me what destiny	E che riserbasi
Holds for one student?	Allo studente?

PREZIOSILLA
(reading his hand)

Anguish and misery, Grief and despair.	Oh, tu miserrime Vicende avrai.

STUDENT

What's that?	Che di'?

PREZIOSILLA
(looking into his face)

I never tell a lie ...	Non mente Il labbro mai ...

(aside)

But you ... young gentleman, You don't deceive me ... You're not a student. I'll not betray you, no, no, no. But I could tell them What you are, tra la la là! Yes, I could tell them What you are, tra la la là!	Ma a te ... carissimo, Non presto fe' ... Non sei studente ... Non dirò niente, no, no, no. Ma gnaffe, a me, Non se la fa, tra la la là! Ma gnaffe, a me, Non se la fa, tra la la là!

Scene Three. *Pilgrims pass by outside in procession. / No. 9 Prayer*

CHORUS OF PILGRIMS
(in the distance)

Holy Father on high,	1° Padre Eterno Signor ...	
Oh hear me cry!	2°	Pietà di noi.
Holy Saviour on high,	1° Divin Figlio Signor ...	
Oh hear me cry!	2°	Pietà di noi.
Holy Spirit on high,	1° Santo Spirto Signor ...	
Oh hear me cry!	2°	Pietà di noi.
Three-in-One, holy Lord,	1° Uno e Trino Signor ...	
Oh hear me cry!	1°	Pietà di noi.

ALL
(As the student rises respectfully.)

Who are they?	Chi sono? ...

ALCALDE

The pilgrims Come for tomorrow's celebration.	Son pellegrini Che vanno al giubileo.

LEONORA
(reappearing in agitation at the door)

(Can I escape him?)	(Fuggir potessi!)

ALL

We'll wait till they have passed us.	Che passino attendiamo.

ALCALDE

And join the prayer.	Preghiam con lor.

CHORUS

Let's pray now.	Preghiamo.

ALL
(leaving the table and kneeling)

To all who kneel before Thee here, Extend Thy hand, O Saviour, From Satan and damnation Oh save us, mighty Lord.	Su noi prostrati e supplici Stendi la man, Signore; Dall'infernal malore Ne salvi tua bontà.

LEONORA

(Ah, from my brother rescue me, So eager to take my life!	(Ah, dal fratello salvami Che anela il sangue mio;

Ah, rescue me, almighty Lord!   Se tu nol vuoi, gran Dio,
Ah, Thou alone canst save me!)   Nessun mi salverà!)

Scene Nine. *Leonora returns to her room and shuts the door behind her. The others resume*
their places: the wine-jug goes round. / No. 10 Scena

STUDENT

Long life to all my good companions!   Viva la buona compagnia!

ALL

Viva!   Viva!

STUDENT
(raising his glass)

Good health on earth, and glory when   Salute qui, l'eterna gloria poi . . .
we die . . .

ALL
(doing the same)

We say Amen.   Cosi sia.

STUDENT

With the angels still, Trabuco?   Già cogli angioli, Trabuco?

TRABUCO

Some hope in all this racket!   E che? con questo inferno!

STUDENT

And did that little person that you brought   E quella personcina con lei giunta,
here
Come for the celebration?   Venne pel giubileo?

TRABUCO

Don't know.   Nol so.

STUDENT

Was he,   Per altro
Or was she, a goose or gander?   È gallo, oppur gallina?

TRABUCO

I didn't look, I only took my payment.   De' viaggiator non bado che al denaro.

STUDENT

You're very prudent!   Molto prudente!
(turning to the Alcalde)
But you saw   Ed Ella
That traveller who came here . . . Why did   Che giungere la vide . . . perchè a cena
he not come
To dine?   Non vien?

ALCALDE

No notion.   L'ignoro.

STUDENT

Doubtless ordered   Dissero chiedesse
Vinegar and water . . . Ha! Ha! As a   Acqua ed aceto . . . Ah! Ah! per rinfrescarsi.
refreshment!

ALCALDE

Could be!   Sarà.

STUDENT

I'm told that he's young and still   E ver ch'è gentile, e senza barba?
quite beardless.

72

ALCALDE

I know nothing.   Non so nulla.

STUDENT

(And you won't tell!)   (Parlar non vuol.)
(to Trabuco)
So back   Ancora
To you; did your companion ride   A lei; stava sul mulo
Side-saddle or astride?   Seduta o a cavalcioni?

TRABUCO
(irritated)

You bore me!   Che noia!

STUDENT

Where did he come from?   Onde veniva?

TRABUCO
(rising)

All I know's that I'm sure to go to Heaven.   So che andrò presto o tardi in paradiso.

STUDENT

Why so?   Perchè?

TRABUCO

You supply my purgatory   Ella il purgatorio
Here below.   Mi fa soffrir ...

STUDENT

Where are you going?   Or dove va? ...

TRABUCO

To the stable,   In istalla
To sleep beside my mules,   A dormir colle mie mule,
They don't know any Latin,   Che non sanno di latino,
I will sleep beside my mules,   A dormir colle mie mule,
They have never been to college.   Che non sono baccellieri.

(He takes his pack-saddle and goes out.)

ALL

Ha! Ha! He's escaped you!   Ah! ah! è fuggito!

Scene Four. *The same without Trabuco. / (No. 10) Ballata*

STUDENT

While that traveller is sleeping, let's paint   Poich'è imberbe l'incognito, facciamgli
On his cheeks a pair of whiskers,   Col nero due baffetti,
And laugh at him tomorrow.   Doman ne rideremo.

CHORUS

Bravo, bravo!   Bravo! Bravo!

ALCALDE

The travellers here are in my care; I forbid it.   Protegger debbo i viaggiator; m'oppongo.
You, sir, had better tell me   Meglio farebbe dirne
Just who you are, where you come from,   Donde venga, ove vada, e chi ella sia.
   and where you're going.

STUDENT

You'd like to know? Then let me tell my   Lo vuol saper? ... Ecco l'istoria mia.
   story.

I'm Pereda, a hardworking student,   [6] Son Pereda, son ricco d'onore,
Got my Bachelors at old Salamanca;   Baccelliere mi fe' Salamanca;
Two more years there and I'll be a doctor,   Sarò presto *in utroque* dottore,

But one year ago I broke off my study ...	Chè di studio ancor poco mi manca ...
My friend Vargas, he asked me to join him,	Di là Vargas mi tolse da un anno,
Leave Salamanca and go to Seville.	E a Siviglia con sè mi guidò.
When he begged me Pereda departed,	Non trattenne Pereda alcun danno,
All he asked me I swore I'd fulfil.	Per l'amico il suo core parlò.
For his sister was wooed by an Indian;	Della suora un amante straniero
Caught in her chamber, her father he murdered;	Colà il padre gli avea trucidato,
My friend Vargas, as honour demanded,	Ed il figlio, da pro' cavaliero,
Swore he'd kill them, revenge his father ...	La vendetta ne aveva giurato ...
So we sought them and traced them to Cadiz,	L'inseguimmo di Cadice in riva,
But no sign could we find of the pair.	Nè la coppia fatal si trovò.
For my Vargas, all of his anguish I swore I would share.	Per l'amico Pereda soffriva,
All of his anguish I swore I would share.	Chè il suo core per esso parlò.
Rumour told us at last that his sister	Là e dovunque narrar che del pari
Fell a victim and died like her father;	La sedotta col vecchio peria,
In the darkness the servants were fighting,	Che a una zuffa tra servi e sicari
But the Indian seducer escaped them.	Solo il vil seduttore sfuggia.
From Don Vargas I soon then was parted,	Io da Vargas allor mi staccava;
For that Indian he swore he would find.	Ei seguir l'assassino giurò.
To America he sailed o'er the ocean,	Verso America il mare solcava,
And Pereda was left here behind!	E Pereda a' suoi studi tornò.

ALL

Dreadful story Pereda has told us!	Truce storia Pereda narrava!
His behaviour was generous and kind.	Generoso il suo cor si mostrò!

No. 11 Scena, Chorus and Reprise of the Dance

ALCALDE

Well spoken.	Sta bene.

PREZIOSILLA
(slyly)

And so that Marquis was murdered?	Ucciso — fu quel Marchese?

STUDENT

He was.	Ebben?

PREZIOSILLA

And the assassin went off with his daughter?	L'amante — rapia sua figlia?

STUDENT

Yes.	Sì.

PREZIOSILLA

And you Pereda, true friend of Vargas,	E voi l'amico — fido, cortese,
When he requested you, went with him to Cadiz?	Andaste a Cadice — e pria a Siviglia? ...
Ah! But I could tell them who you are.	Ah, gnaffe, a me — non se la fa ...
Tra la la là!	Tra la la là!

ALCALDE
(getting up and looking at the clock)

My friends, it's late now; now that we have eaten	Figliuoli, è tardi; poichè abbiam cenato
Let's give our thanks to God and be gone.	Si rendan grazie a Dio, e partiam ...

ALL

We'll go.	Partiamo.

ALCALDE

Good night now!	Or buona notte.

ALL

Good night now.	Buona notte.
Hola! Hola!	Holà! Holà!
The time has come to part.	Allegri, o mulattier!
O merry muleteer, our work is done!	È l'ora di posar.
To one and all good night.	Andiam, andiam, andiam.

(*They leave.*)

Scene Five. *A small plateau on a steep mountainside. To the right are ravines and boulders; in the centre the poor and humble facade of the church of Our Lady of the Angels; to the left is the door of the monastery, in the middle of which is a little window, and beside which is the bell rope; a small porch projects above it. Beyond the church are high mountains and the village of Hornachuelos. The door to the church is closed but above it light shines through a wide semicircular window. In the middle of the stage, a little to the left, an old stone cross, weather-beaten by time, stands at the top of four steps. Clearest moonlight illuminates the scene.*

Donna Leonora comes up from the right, exhausted, clothed as a man, in a wide-sleeved pilgrim's cloak, a broad-brimmed hat and boots. / No. 12 Aria [1]

LEONORA

I'm safe here! . . . God, I thank Thee!	Son giunta! . . . grazie, o Dio!
In this retreat I'll end my days! . . . I've reached it! . . .	Estremo asil quest'è per me! . . . son giunta! . . .
I tremble! . . . They know my fearful story,	Io tremo! . . . la mia orrenda storia è nota
They heard it in the tavern . . . my brother dared to tell them!	In quell'albergo . . . e mio fratel narrolla! . . .
If he learned of my presence! . . . Fatal! . . . He said	Se scoperta m'avesse! . . . Cielo! . . . Ei disse
Alvaro had sailed away to his native country!	Naviga verso occaso Don Alvaro!
He did not perish on that dread night when	Nè morto cadde quella notte in cui
I, my father's blood still fresh upon me,	Io, io del sangue di mio padre intrisa,
When I followed him and lost him! And now he leaves me	L'ho seguito, e il perdei! ed or mi lascia,
To suffer! Ah! Alas, I cannot bear this anguish!	Mi fugge! ohimè, non reggo a tanta ambascia!

(*falling on her knees*)

Virgin, look down and comfort me,	[7] Madre, pietosa Vergine,
Forgive me I implore you,	Perdona al mio peccato;
Oh, help me to forget him	M'aita quell'ingrato
And drive him from my heart.	Dal core a cancellar.
And here in holy solitude	In queste solitudini
I will atone for my transgression . . .	Espierò l'errore . . .
Oh hear my cry, have mercy Lord . . .	Pietà di me, Signore . . .
Do not forsake me now!	Deh, non m'abbandonar!
I cry to Thee my Saviour,	Pietà di me, Signore . . .
Do not forsake me now!	Deh, non m'abbandonar!

CHORUS OF MONKS
(*off-stage*)

Venite, adoremus et procedamus ante Deum,	*Venite, adoremus et procedamus ante Deum,*
Ploremus coram Domino qui fecit nos.	*Ploremus coram Domino qui fecit nos.*

(*An organ accompanies the monks at matins.*)

LEONORA
(*rising*)

The chanting of the antiphon . . .	Ah, que' sublimi cantici . . .
The organ's solemn music	Dell'organo i concenti,
Like incense is ascending to	Che come incenso ascendono
The sky, to God in Heaven,	A Dio sui firmamenti,
Inspiring me with comfort,	Inspirano a quest'alma
New hope, with new hope and comfort!	Fede, conforto e calma! . . .
I'll go and ask for sanctuary . . .	Al santo asilo accorrasi . . .

(*going to the doorway*)

But dare I ring so early?	E l'oserò a quest'ora?

75

If someone were to find me here!	Alcun potria sorprendermi!
Still cursed by fate, Leonora?	Oh misera Leonora,
Fear not! The pious friar will welcome you,	Tremi? . . . il pio frate accoglierti,
You'll not be turned away.	No, non ricuserà.
Stay by my side, to comfort me,	Non mi lasciar, soccorrimi,
And hear my cry, O Lord.	Pietà, Signor, pietà!

(She goes to ring the monastery bell.)

Scene Six. *Leonora rings the bell; Melitone opens the little window, his lantern throwing light on her face, and frightening her; he converses through the window. / No. 13 Scena*

MELITONE

Who are you?   Chi siete?

LEONORA

I seek the Father Guardian.   Chiedo il Superiore.

MELITONE

Promptly   S'apre

At five we will open,   Alle cinque la chiesa,

To hold the celebration.   Se al giubileo venite.

LEONORA

Find him and call him,   Il Superiore,

For pity's sake.   Per carità.

MELITONE

Pity's asleep till day-break!   Che carità a quest'ora?

LEONORA

I'm sent by Father Cleto.   Mi manda il Padre Cleto.

MELITONE

Now you're talking! What's your business?   Quel sant'uomo? . . . Il motivo?

LEONORA

It's urgent.   Urgente.

MELITONE

Tell me more . . .   Perchè mai? . . .

LEONORA

A wretched sinner . . .   Un infelice . . .

MELITONE

Same old story. Step inside for a moment!   Brutta solfa, però v'apro ond'entriate.

LEONORA

I dare not.   Nol posso.

MELITONE

No? An excommunication?   No? . . . Scomunicato siete?

It's very odd you should choose to wait   Che strano fia aspettar a ciel sereno.
    outside here!

I'll call him . . . and if I don't come back,   V'annuncio . . . e se non torno

Goodnight sir!   Buona notte . . .

(He shuts the window.)

Scene Seven. *Leonora alone.*

LEONORA

But what if he refuses . . .   Ma s'ei mi respingesse! . . .

All men have said he's kindly . . .   Fama pietoso il dice . . .

He'll shelter me today ... Virgin, oh help me.

Ei mi proteggerà ... Vergin, m'assisti, m'assisti.

Scene Eight. *Leonora, Father Guardiano, Brother Melitone. / No. 14 Scena and Duet*

GUARDIANO

Who requires me?

Chi mi cerca?

LEONORA

A pilgrim.

Son io.

GUARDIANO

Tell me.

Dite.

LEONORA

It is secret.

Un segreto ...

GUARDIANO

Then leave us, Melitone.

Andate, Meliton.

MELITONE
(*leaving*)

(A secret session!
A new confession! And reserved for the prior!
The rest of us are far too frail
To listen to a spicy tale.)

(Sempre segreti!
E questi santi soli han da saperli!
Noi siamo tanti cavoli,
Noi siamo tanti cavoli ...)

GUARDIANO

My brother,
Were you mumbling?

Fratello,
Mormorate?

MELITONE

Oh no, merely said the hinges
Are rusty, they need oiling ...

Oibò, dico ch'è pesante
La porta, e fa rumore ...

GUARDIANO

Then obey me.

Obbedite ...

MELITONE

(He's far too high and mighty!)

(Che tuon da superiore!)

(*He retires into the monastery, noisily closing the door.*)

Scene Nine. *Leonora and Father Guardiano.*

GUARDIANO

We're alone here.

Or siam soli ...

LEONORA

Then a woman entreats you.

Una donna so io.

GUARDIANO

All alone here at this hour! Great Heaven!

Una donna a quest'ora! ... Gran Dio!

LEONORA

I'm unhappy, deserted, accursed,
And rejected by earth and by Heaven,
I implore you in mercy to save me,
For the torments of Satan await me.

[8] Infelice, delusa, reietta,
Dalla terra e dal ciel maledetta,
Che nel pianto, prostratavi al piede,
Di sottrarla all'inferno vi chiede.

GUARDIANO

Can a poor humble friar be of use?

Come un povero frate lo può?

77

LEONORA

Father Cleto has told you my tale?	Padre Cleto un suo foglio v'inviò?

GUARDIANO

Did he send you?	Ei vi manda?

LEONORA

Yes.	Si.

GUARDIANO
(*surprised*)

So then you must be	Dunque voi siete
Leonora de Vargas!	Leonora di Vargas!

LEONORA

You shudder!	Fremete! . . .

GUARDIANO

No . . . But kneel by the cross of our Saviour,	No . . . Venite fidente alla croce,
There kind Heaven will calmly inspire you.	Là del cielo v'ispiri la voce.

LEONORA
(*She kneels by the cross, kisses it devoutly and turns again to face him.*)

How my sorrow has been lightened	[9] Più tranquilla l'alma sento
Since I sought this holy ground here;	Dacchè premo questa terra;
Here no longer am I frightened,	De' fantasmi lo spavento
Evil spirits are not found here . . .	Più non provo farmi guerra . . .
And no more I see the spectre	Più non sorge sanguinante
Of my father rise in fury;	Di mio padre l'ombra innante;
And the daughter's ear no longer	Nè terribile l'ascolto
Hears a father's dying curse.	La sua figlia maledir.

GUARDIANO

At Our Lady of the Angels,	Sempre indarno qui rivolto
Satan strives in vain to dwell.	Fu di Satana l'ardir.

LEONORA

For that reason I would die here,	Perciò tomba qui desio,
Where that other woman perished.	Fra le rupi ov'altra visse.

GUARDIANO

What! You know that?	Che! . . . Sapete?

LEONORA

Cleto told me.	Cleto il disse . . .

GUARDIANO

You're decided?	E volete?

LEONORA

God has called me!	Darmi a Dio.

GUARDIANO

But beware if you are led astray	Guai per chi si lascia illudere
By your grief and your confusion!	Dal delirio d'un momento!
You are young, and what you swear today	Più fatal per voi si giovane
May bring cruel disillusion.	Giungerebbe il pentimento . . .
Who can read the clouded future	[10] Chi può legger nel futuro,
Or be certain of his heart?	Chi immutabil farvi il cor?
And your lover?	E l'amante?

LEONORA

By fatal accident	Involontario
He took my father's life.	Di mio padre è l'uccisor.

GUARDIANO	
And your brother?	E il fratello?

LEONORA

He has sworn	La mia morte
That by his hand his sister dies.	Di sua mano egli giurò.

GUARDIANO

You were best to seek salvation	Meglio a voi le sante porte
In a convent.	Schiuda un chiostro.

LEONORA

A convent? No.	Un chiostro? . . . No.
If you abandon this wretched sinner,	Se voi scacciate questa pentita
Then on the mountains I'll howl for mercy;	Andrò per balze gridando aita,
On moor and mountain I'll seek a refuge,	Ricovrò ai monti, cibo alle selve,
Until the beasts come to end my woe.	E fin le belve — ne avran pietà.
A voice from Heaven softly was calling:	Ah sì, del cielo qui udii la voce:
'Here is the Cross, the Cross that will save you.'	Salvati all'ombra di questa croce . . .
And you reject me? Here lies salvation,	Voi mi scacciate? È questo il porto;

(She runs and clings to the cross.)

Can you deny me, or bar my way?	Chi tal conforto — mi toglierà?

GUARDIANO

(To Thee be glory, Father Almighty,	[11] (A te sia gloria, o Dio clemente,
Granting to all who grieve Thy consolation,	Padre dei miseri onnipossente,
Thou whom the earth and heavens obey,	A cui sgabello sono le sfere! . . .
Oh, may Thy will be done today.)	Il tuo volere — si compirà!)
You are decided?	È fermo il voto? . . .

LEONORA

Decided.	È fermo.

GUARDIANO

God in grace receive you!	V'accolga dunque Iddio . . .

LEONORA

Divine salvation!	Bontà divina!

GUARDIANO

Your name shall be a secret . . .	Sol io saprò chi siete . . .
There's a cave in the mountains, there find your refuge.	Tra le rupi e uno speco; ivi starete.
Streams give you water, and once every week	Presso una fonte al settimo di scarso
I myself will provide your food.	Cibo porròvvi io stesso.

LEONORA

I go there . . .	V'andiamo . . .

GUARDIANO
(turning towards the door)

Melitone? . . .	Melitone? . . .

(to Melitone as he joins them)

Call all the friars, tell them to assemble,	Tutti i fratelli con ardenti ceri,
Let each friar light a candle,	Dov'è l'ara maggiore,
And bear it in procession to the altar.	Nel tempio si raccolgan del Signore . . .

(Melitone goes in.)

At morning light you'll seek that cave,	[12] Sull'alba il piede all'eremo
The path lies clear before you;	Solinga volgerete;
But first receive the sacred Host	Ma pria dal pane angelico
To comfort and restore you.	Conforto all'alma avrete.
So don the garb of poverty,	Le sante lane a cingere
Go, do not be afraid.	Ite, e sia forte il cor.

Recall that on your lonely way The Lord will lend you aid.	Sul nuovo calle a reggervi V'assisterà il Signor.

LEONORA
(reassured)

O Father, I thank Thee, Thou smil'st on this poor sinner! A new hope inspires my soul! I know I am forgiven! I feel my life begin once more, My courage is restored. Rejoice with me angelic host, I'm rescued by the Lord.	[13] Tua grazia, o Dio, Sorride alla reietta! Mel dice un gaudio insolito. Io son ribenedetta! Già sento in me rinascere A nuova vita il cor ... Plaudite, o cori angelici, Mi perdonò il Signor.

(They go in through the porter's door.)

Scene Ten. *The great door of the church opens. Ahead the high altar is illuminated. The organ plays. The chorus assembles in two long files of friars, carrying lighted candles, and kneeling on either side. Father Guardiano precedes Leonora (dressed as a friar); he leads her out of the church, followed by the friars who take up positions around them. Leonora prostrates herself before him as he solemnly raises his hands above her head and intones. / No. 15 Second Finale*

GUARDIANO

Almighty Father who reads every secret, Thy name be blessed.	Il santo nome di Dio Signore Sia benedetto.

ALL

Now and for ever.	Sia benedetto.

GUARDIANO

A wretched sinner repents of his error, Here in our mountains he seeks a shelter. The holy cave to him shall be opened. You know the place?	Un'alma a piangere — viene l'errore, Fra queste balze — chiede ricetto ... [14] Il santo speco — noi le schiudiamo ... V'è noto il loco?

ALL

We know the place.	Lo conosciam.

GUARDIANO

The hermit's refuge must be respected — Let none approach it.	A quest'asilo — sacro inviolato Nessun si appressi.

ALL

We shall obey.	Obbedirem.

GUARDIANO

The humble precinct hard by the cavern — No foot may cross it.	Il cinto umile — non sia varcato Che nel divide.

ALL

None shall approach.	Nol varcherem.

GUARDIANO

And if a rash man breaks my commandment, Or would discover the name or story Of him who dwells there, he is accursed.	A chi il divieto — franger osasse O di quest'alma — scoprir tentasse Nome o mistero, — maledizione!

ALL

He is accursed, he is accursed! May Heaven strike him down with fiery lightning, Flame destroy the intruder who dares to enter; Oh may the elements be loosed upon him ... And may his impious dust by wind be scattered.	Maledizione! Maledizione! Il cielo fulmini, — incenerisca L'empio mortale — se tanto ardisca; Su lui scateni — ogni elemento ... L'immonda cenere — ne sperda il vento.

Prepare yourself, you must leave us. Alone and silent
Live in repentance. There's a bell by which
You can call us if by danger you are threatened,
Or, in the hour when your death approaches . . .
Then we will bring you comfort
For your soul before it goes to meet its Creator.

Alzatevi e partite. Alcun vivente
Più non vedrete. Dello speco il bronzo
Ne avverta se periglio vi sovrasti,
O per voi giunto sia l'estremo giorno . . .
A confortarvi l'alma
Volerem, pria ch'a Dio faccia ritorno.

ALL

The blessed Virgin pray for thee,
Beneath her mantle hide thee,
May God protect thy lonely way
With guardian angels beside thee.

[15] La Vergine degli Angeli
Vi copra del suo manto,
E voi protegga vigile
Di Dio l'angelo santo.

(All, with Leonora, repeat this hymn. Then Leonora kisses Father Guardiano's hand and departs alone for her hermitage. The friars extinguish their candles and reenter the church in the same order. Father Guardiano stops at the door, with his hand raised in an attitude of blessing in the direction of Leonora's exit.)

The curtain falls.

Design by Palanti for Melitone, La Scala, 1908 (Museo Teatrale alla Scala)

Act Three

In Italy, near Velletri *

Scene One. *Woodland: dark night: voices off – stage right – of soldiers playing cards. Don Alvaro in a captain's uniform of the Royal Grenadiers appears at the back, deep in thought. /* No. 16 *Gamblers' Chorus, Scena and Romanza*

VOICES

So deal the cards round, attention!	Attenti al gioco, attenti,
Yes, deal the cards round, attention!	Attenti al gioco, attenti!
I lead an ace then! It's my trick!	Un asso a destra. Ho vinto.
Then deal a new round, attention!	Attenti al gioco, attenti . . .
A three of diamonds . . . Five to beat it. Your trick!	Un tre a destra . . . Cinque a manca. Perdo.
Attention, attention!	Attenti, attenti!

ALVARO
(sadly, but forcefully)

For one like me, all life is torment. But vainly	La vita è inferno all'infelice . . . Invano
Death I have courted! Seville, Leonora!	Morte desio! . . . Siviglia! . . . Leonora! . . .
Cruel remembrance! Oh night	Oh rimembranze! . . . Oh notte
That robbed my life of its every joy!	Ch'ogni ben mi rapisti! . . .
And fate decrees that I must suffer for ever.	Sarò infelice eternamente . . . è scritto.
My father tried to free his native country	Della natal sua terra il padre volle
From Spanish persecution, and so he wed	Spezzar l'estranio giogo, e coll'unirsi
The last of all the Incas, and he hoped to	All'ultima degl'Incas la corona
Gain the Peruvian crown. A vain endeavour!	Cingerne confidò . . . Fu vana impresa!
I was born in a prison; spent my youth	In un carcere nacqui; m'educava
In the desert; I live because no Spaniard	Il deserto; sol vivo perchè ignota
Knows my royal lineage! . . . My noble parents,	È mia regale stirpe! . . . I miei parenti
Who dreamed of a kingdom, died on a Spanish scaffold! . . .	Sognarono un trono e li destò la scure! . . .
Oh God, is there no end to all my suffering?	Oh, quando fine avran le mie sventure?
High in the realms of paradise,	[16] O tu che in seno agl' angeli,
Far from this mortal prison,	Eternamente pura
Blessed by eternal loveliness,	Salisti bella, incolume
Robed in the light of Heaven,	Dalla mortal jattura,
Look down upon my anguish,	Non iscordar di volgere
And pity my keen sorrow,	Un guardo a me tapino,
A nameless exiled wanderer	Chè senza nome ed esule,
By destiny pursued;	In odio del destino,
My only hope, ah misery,	Chiedo anelando, ahi misero,
Is death to end my pain . . .	La morte d'incontrar . . .
Leonora, hear me, pray for me,	Leonora mia, soccorrimi,
Look down in mercy I pray.	Pietà del mio penar.

No. 17 Scena and Duettino

CARLOS
(off-stage)

I caught you cheating . . .	Al tradimento . . .

VOICES

Kill him!	Muoia . . .

ALVARO

Who is shouting?	Quali grida!

---

* During the War of the Austrian Succession (1740-48) the Spanish, assisted by the King of Naples, drove the Austrians out of much of Southern Italy.

CARLOS

Come help me!

Aita ...

ALVARO

I will help you!

Si soccorra.

VOICES

Kill the Spaniard.

Muoia, muoia ...

(*He runs in the direction of the cry: the clash of weapons is heard: some soldiers cross the stage, running in disorder from the right to the left.*)

Scene Two. *Don Alvaro returns with Carlos.*

ALVARO

They fled! But were you wounded?

Fuggir! ... ferito siete?

CARLOS

No, for you came
To save me.

La vita.

No, vi debbo

ALVARO

Who were those men?

Chi erano?

CARLOS

Assassins.

Assassini.

ALVARO

But so close
To the camp?

Al campo cosi?

Presso

CARLOS

Let me confess,
A gambling quarrel ...

Franco
Dirò; fu alterco al gioco ...

ALVARO

I see now. And they were cheating?

Comprendo, colà, a destra?

CARLOS

Yes.

Si.

ALVARO

But tell me:
How could a Spanish captain get involved
With such rabble?

Ma come
Si nobile d'aspetto, a quella bisca
Scendeste?

CARLOS

I am new here,
Arrived here last night with despatches
from our general;
But for you I would be dead.
Please tell me to whom I'm indebted?

Nuovo sono.
Con ordini del general sol ieri
Giunsi; senza voi, morto
Sarei. Or dite a chi debbo la vita?

ALVARO

To fortune ...

Al caso ...

CARLOS

Then let me give you my name
(The name I've taken):
Don Felice de Bornos, aide-de-camp to
Our general ...

Pria il mio nome
Dirò (non sappia il vero):
Don Felice de Bornos, aiutante
Del Duce ...

ALVARO

I'm Captain of the Grenadiers;
Don Federico Herreros.

Io Capitan de' Granatieri,
Don Federico Herreros.

CARLOS

The hero of the regiment!	La gloria dell'esercito!

ALVARO

I beg you . . .	Signore . . .

CARLOS

I'd like to make your friendship, if you, sir, will grant it.	Io l'amistà ne ambia, la chiedo e spero.

ALVARO

If I could claim your friendship I'd be honoured.	Io pure della vostra sarò fiero.

(They clasp their right hands.)

BOTH

United, we fight together,	Amici in vita e in morte
Companions until my dying breath . . .	Il mondo ne vedrà . . .
United, we fight together	Uniti in vita e in morte
In triumph, or in death . . .	Entrambi troverà.
United, comrades in battle,	Uniti in vita e in morte
Companions in life or death.	Entrambi troverà.

VOICES
(off-stage, with trumpets blaring)

To battle!	All'armi!

CARLOS AND ALVARO

Companion . . . to battle!	Andiamo . . . all'armi!

CARLOS

I'll advance to the field at your side,	Con voi scendere al campo d'onor,
Give your orders and I will obey.	Emularne l'esempio potrò.

ALVARO

Don Felice, with you at my side,	Testimone del vostro valor,
I'll admire your valour today.	Ammirarne le prove saprò.

(They run off to the left.)

Scene Three. *Morning: the anteroom of the officers' quarters of senior Spanish staff in Italy, near Velletri. Two doors at the back, one leading to a bedroom, the other to a common-room, etc.. A window left. Noise of the battle in progress. / No. 18 Scena and Battle*

An army surgeon and some orderlies enter through the main door and run to the window.

ORDERLIES

Fierce is the battle! . . .	Arde la mischia! . . .

SURGEON
(looking through a telescope)

Grenadiers advancing!	Prodi i granatieri!

ORDERLIES

Herreros leads them . . .	Li guida Herreros . . .

SURGEON

Ah!   Ciel!

He has been wounded! . . . They leave him	Ferito ei cade! . . . Piegano
Lying . . . but his comrade	I suoi! . . . l'aiutante
Has recalled them . . . and they rally at his orders!	Li raccozza . . . alla carica li guida!
The enemy are defeated! . . . And we're victorious!	Già fuggono i nemici*! i nostri han vinto!

---

* 1862: i Tedeschi — 'the Germans'. Altered in the 1869 score.

Hurrah for Spain!   A Spagna gloria!

OTHERS

And Italia!   Viva l'Italia!

ALL

Victorious!   Vittoria!

SURGEON

Now they bring the wounded captain here.   Portan qui ferito il capitan.

Scene Four. *Four grenadiers carry on Don Alvaro, wounded, on a stretcher: beside it the surgeon and Don Carlos, dust-stained from battle and in much anxiety. A soldier puts down the wounded man's valise on a side-table. The stretcher is lowered. / No. 19 Scena and Duettino*

CARLOS

Slowly and gently . . . for he is gravely   Piano . . . qui posi . . . approntisi il mio
    wounded.   letto.

SURGEON

No talking . . .   Silenzio . . .

CARLOS

Is there danger?   V'ha periglio?

SURGEON

The bullet in his chest may be fatal.   La palla che ha nel petto mi spaventa.

CARLOS

Try to save him.   Deh, il salvate.

ALVARO
(*regaining consciousness*)

Where am I?   Ove son?

CARLOS

Close to your comrade.   Presso l'amico.

ALVARO

Then gladly I can die here.   Lasciatemi morire.

CARLOS

You will not die, for we can save you . . .   Vi salveran le nostre cure . . . Premio
Your reward will be the Star of Calatrava.   L'ordine vi sarà di Calatrava.

ALVARO
(*starting violently*)

Of Calatrava! No, never!   Di Calatrava! . . . mai . . . mai . . .

CARLOS

(Ah! Why should the name of Calatrava   (Che! inorridi di Calatrava al nome!)
    appal him?)

ALVARO

My comrade . . .   Amico . . .

SURGEON

No more talking . . .   Se parlate . . .

ALVARO

Just one last word . . .   Un detto sol . . .

CARLOS
(to the surgeon)

Please leave us for a moment . . .   Ven prego, ne lasciate . . .

(The surgeon retires to the back.)

ALVARO
(beckoning Don Carlos to him)

In death's solemn moment, oh grant me   [17] Solenne in quest'ora giurarmi dovete
one favour,
And do what I ask you.   Far pago un mio voto.

CARLOS
(with emotion)

I swear it.   Lo giuro.

ALVARO

Then feel in   Sul core

My tunic . . .   Cercate . . .

CARLOS
(finding a key inside the tunic)

There's a key here!   Una chiave! . . .

ALVARO
(pointing to his valise)

It opens a secret,   Con essa trarrete

Concealed in my papers . . . I trust in your   Un piego celato . . . l'affido all'onore . . .
honour
For they hold a mystery, with me it must   Colà v'ha un mistero, che meco morrà.
die.
So swear you will burn them . . .   S'abbruci me spento . . .

CARLOS

I swear it, I swear.   Lo giurò, sarà.

ALVARO

Now I die contented . . . My friend – I   Or muoio tranquillo. Vi stringo al cor mio.
embrace you . . .

CARLOS
(embracing him with emotion)

Herreros, my comrade, have faith now in   Amico, fidate nel cielo. Addio.
Heaven. I leave you.

ALVARO

I leave you.   Addio.

(The surgeon and orderlies carry the wounded man into an adjoining room.)

Scene Five. *Don Carlos, later the surgeon. / No. 20 Scena and Aria*

CARLOS

To die! . . . Tremendous moment! . . .   Morir! . . . tremenda cosa! . . .
So valiant, so noble,   Sì intrepido, sì prode,
Yet he must die! . . . There's something   Ei pur morrà! . . . Uom singolar costui! . . .
strange about him!
The name of Calatrava   Tremò di Calatrava
Shocked him! . . . Has someone told him   Al nome! . . . A lui palese
About my family shame? . . . Heavens! . . .   N'è forse il disonor? . . . Cielo! . . . qual
It can't be! . . .   lampo!
Is he that foul seducer?   S'ei fosse il seduttore? . . .
Here at my mercy . . . alive still!   Desso in mia mano . . . e vive!
If I'm mistaken . . . This key will tell me.   Se m'ingannassi? questa chiave il dica.

(He throws open the valise and takes out a sealed envelope.)

Here are the letters! . . .   Ecco i fogli . . .

(He starts to open it . . .)

86

I cannot!	Che tento!

(. . . but stops himself)

For I swore I'd destroy them! . . . And to his valour	E la fe' che giurai? . . . e questa vita
Today I owe my life. But I saved his life!	Che debbo al suo valor? . . . anch'io lo salvo!
And what if he were that cursed Indian	E s'ei fosse quell'Indo maledetto
Who defiled my family honour?	Che macchiò il sangue mio? . . .

(resolutely)

Let the seal be broken,	Il suggello si franga,

(again about to open the envelope)

No-one can see me . . .	Niun qui mi vede . . .

(He stops himself.)

No? My eyes can see me!	No? . . . Ben mi vegg'io!

(He throws the envelope down, recoiling in horror.)

Ah, fatal mystery, hiding my future, [18]	Urna fatale del mio destino
Get you behind me, in vain you tempt me;	Va, t'allontana, mi tenti invano;
My tarnished honour I came to rescue;	L'onor a terger qui venni, e insano
Can I defile it by new deeds of shame?	D'un' onto nuova nol macchierò.
All vows are sacred to men of honour,	Un giuro è sacro per l'uom d'onore;
So let these papers hold their secret for ever . . .	Que' fogli serbino il lor mistero . . .
Dream of betrayal lure me no longer,	Disperso vada il mal pensiero
That vile temptation to break my vow.	Che all'atto indegno mi concitò.
But what if there are other ways to prove it? . . .	E s'altra prova rinvenir potessi? . . .
I'll see.	Vediam.

(He searches in the valise and finds a locket.)

Here is a portrait . . .	Qui v'ha un ritratto . . .

(He examines it.)

It has no seal . . . he named no portrait . . . I made no Promise . . . Let me look then . . .	Suggel non v'è . . . nulla ei ne disse . . . nulla Promisi . . . S'aprà dunque . . .

(continuing to examine the contents)

Ah! Leonora!	Ciel! Leonora!

(in exaltation)

So he is Don Alvaro!	Don Alvaro è il ferito!
May he recover, so that my sword can kill him! . . .	Ora egli viva . . . e di mia man poi muoia . . .

SURGEON

(appearing, happily, at the door of the room)

He will recover,* I've saved him.	Lieta novella,* è salvo.

(He enters.)

CARLOS

You saved him! I triumph!	Oh gioia! oh gioia!
He is safe! And joy of vengeance	Egli è salvo! oh gioia immensa
Fills my heart with keen elation!	Che m'innondi il cor, ti sento!
Now at last on that betrayer	Potrò alfine il tradimento
I'll avenge my father's name.	Sull'infame vendicar.
Leonora, shall I find you?	Leonora, ove t'ascondi? . . .
Did you come to seek your lover,	Di': seguisti tra le squadre
Did you join this army rabble, boldly painted	Chi del sangue di tuo padre
Like a harlot with your dying father's blood?	Ti fe' il volto rosseggiar?
Ah! My joy will be completed	Ah, felice appien sarei
If I find them both together,	Se potesse il brando mio
And my sword can swiftly slay them,	Amendue d'averno al Dio,
Send them both to hell below!	D'un sol colpo consacrar!

(He hurries out to the right.)

---

* 1862: Here is the bullet / Ecco la palla

Scene Six. *A military camp near Velletri; down-stage left, a booth for second-hand goods, another up right where they sell provisions, drinks and fruit. All around are soldiers' tents, stalls for second-hand goods etc.. It is night and the stage is empty. / No. 21 Patrol Chorus (Ronda)**

A patrol enters cautiously, spying out the land.

CHORUS

Companions, be silent!	Compagni, sostiamo;
We'll stop here a moment;	Il campo esploriamo;
I don't hear a sound.	Non s'ode rumore.
The camp is in darkness,	Non brilla un chiarore;
No creature is stirring,	In sonno profondo
They're all sleeping sound.	Sepolto ognun sta.
And leave them to slumber,	Compagni, inoltriamo,

(further off and disappearing)

For only too early	Fra poco la sveglia
Reveille will sound.	Suonare s'udrà.

Scene Seven. *The day slowly dawns. Enter Don Alvaro, deep in thought. / No. 22 Scena and Duet*

ALVARO

Cruel fate still denies me	Nè gustare m'è dato
One single hour of comfort. My soul is weary	Un'ora di quiete; affranta è l'alma
Of the struggle with fate. Peace and oblivion	Dalla lotta crudel. Pace ed oblio
Are all I long for; I pray to Heaven . . . unanswered!	Indarno io chieggo al cielo. Indarno, indarno, indarno.

Scene Eight. *The same and Don Carlos.*

CARLOS

Captain . . .	Capitan . . .

ALVARO

Who requires me?	Chi mi chiama?

(Approaching and recognizing Carlos, he greets him affectionately.)

You? You whose care and kindness	Voi che si larghe cure
Saved me and cured me!	Mi prodigaste?

CARLOS

So your wound has mended	La ferita vostra
And you're recovered?	Sanata è appieno? †

ALVARO

Yes.	Sì.

CARLOS

Fully?	Forte?

ALVARO

Completely.	Qual prima.

---

* This Patrol Chorus was added in 1869. In 1862, the Act moved directly to the chorus 'Drums and fifes' (No. 23) on page 92, and continued with the varied scenes of military life. The second Alvaro-Carlos duet followed the Rataplan.

† The 1862 Act Three Scene Eleven began here, with these lines:

ALVARO

The care that you bestowed on me has cured me.	E come ricambiarvi tante cure?

CARLOS

Quite well again?	Rimesso appien?

88

Could you fight in a duel?   Sosterreste un duel?

ALVARO

        With whom?   E con chi mai?

CARLOS

Do you not have an enemy?   Nemici non avete?

ALVARO

Everyone has . . . but my comrade, I scarce   Tutti ne abbiam . . . ma a stento
Understand you . . .   Comprendo . . .

CARLOS

    No? You're slow to understand me,   No? . . . Messaggio non v'inviava
Don Alvaro the Indian?   Don Alvaro l'Indiano?

ALVARO

      So you betrayed me?   Oh tradimento!
Disloyal! You have broken a vow that was [19] Sleale! il segreto fu dunque violato?
sacred?

CARLOS

No vow have I broken, the portrait betrayed   Fu illeso quel piego, l'effige ha parlato;
  you;
Don Carlos de Vargas, now tremble,   Don Carlo di Vargas, tremate, io sono.
  behold me!

ALVARO

But why should I tremble? Your threat   D'ardite minacce non m'agito al suono.
cannot move me.

CARLOS

Then draw for a duel, and pay what you   Usciamo all'istante, un deve morire . . .
owe me . . .

ALVARO

To die is a trifle, but how can I duel   La morte disprezzo, ma duolmi inveire
With someone who offered me friendship   Contr'uom che per primo amistade m'offria.
  for ever?

CARLOS

No, no, profanation to call me friend.   No, no, profanato tal nome non sia.

ALVARO

Not I, it was destiny that slayed your father; Non io, fu il destino, che il padre v'ha ucciso,
Leonora was spotless, that angel of virtue . . . Non io che sedussi quell'angiol d'amore . . .
They gaze down together, both in Heaven   Ne guardano entrambi, e dal paradiso
  united,
Declaring I am blameless; can your heart   Ch'io sono innocente vi dicono al core . . .
  not hear them? . . .

CARLOS

Go on with your tale!   Adunque colei?

ALVARO

     The night when I lost her,   La notte fatale
And lost all I lived for, I fell gravely wounded; Io caddi per doppia ferita mortale;
When healed at last, a year long I sought   Guaritone, un anno in traccia ne andai.
  her in vain.
Alas, I discovered Leonora was dead.   Ahimè, ch'era spenta Leonora trovai.

CARLOS

You're lying, you're lying!   Menzogna, menzogna!

In vain you endeavour to calm all the fury,	* Invano calmare, tentate le furie,
That fires my heart to vengeance.	Che straziano il core.
In Heaven I can hear him, my father, proclaiming:	Dal cielo ti sento, o padre, gridare:
'Revenge me, revenge me, your honour demands it!'	'Vendetta, vendetta! L'esige l'onore!'
My sister found refuge with one of our kinsmen;	La suora ospitava la antica parente:
I followed, too late . . .	Vi giunsi, ma tardi . . .

ALVARO
(anxiously)

Leonora?	Ed ella . . .

CARLOS

Escaped me.	Fuggente.

ALVARO
(starting in amazement)

Alive still! Don Carlos, this sudden joy	E vive!!! o amico, il fremito
That fills my spirit, and makes me tremble,	Ch'ogni mia fibra scuote,
Must tell you that my heart is true,	Vi dica che quest'anima
That I am free from baseness . . .	Infame esser non puote . . .
Living! O God, I thank you!	Vive!!! gran Dio, quell'angelo . . .

CARLOS

She lives still.	Ella vive,
When I find her she will die.	Ma in breve morirà.

ALVARO

No, we'll fulfil that sacred vow	[20] No, d'un imene il vincolo
By which our hearts were plighted;	Stringa fra noi la speme;
If she is living, united	E s'ella vive, insieme
We'll find her where she has fled.	Cerchiamo ove fuggi.
I swear my blood is noble too,	Giuro che illustre origine
Equal to yours in splendour;	Eguale a voi mi rende,
I am no base pretender,	E che il mio stemma splende
Proudly I bear my noble name.	Come rifulge il di.

CARLOS

Madman! Blood of my father	Stolto! fra noi dischiudesi
Ever parts us from each other;	Insanguinato avello:
How can I call you brother	Come chiamar fratello
Who brought on me this shame?	Chi tutto mi rapi?
Of vile or noble lineage,	D'eccelsa o vile origine.
My honour bids me slay you,	È d'uopo ch'io vi spegna.
And after you, to slay her,	E dopo voi l'indegna
The sister who soiled our name.	Che il sangue suo tradi.

ALVARO

You'd kill her?	Che dite?

CARLOS

Yes, she will die.	Ella morrà.

ALVARO

Be silent!	Tacete.

CARLOS

I swear to God	Il giuro
That my sword will kill her!	A Dio! morrà l'infame.

---

* The four lines that follow were omitted in the 1869 revision.

ALVARO

You first shall perish in our mortal combat!

Voi pria cadrete nel fatal certame.

CARLOS

Fight me! And if my life is granted me,
My sword shall have no rest,
When at last I find Leonora,
I shall drive it in her breast.

Morte! ov'io non cada esangue
Leonora giungerò.
Tinto ancor del vostro sangue
Questo acciar le immergerò.

ALVARO

Die first! Yes! My sword shall slay you
And a murderer now shall die.
So prepare your soul for Heaven;
Say a prayer to God on high.

Morte, sì! . . . col brando mio
Un sicario ucciderò;
Il pensier volgete a Dio,
L'ora vostra alfin suonò.

(*They draw swords and fight furiously.*)*

Scene Nine. *Members of the patrol run up and separate them.*

CHORUS

Stop them! Arrest them!

Fermi, arrestate!

CARLOS
(*furiously resisting*)

No. It is his life
Or mine . . . Leave us.

No. La sua vita
O la mia . . . tosto.

CHORUS

Go fight your duel
Elsewhere.

Lunge di qua
Si tragga.

ALVARO

(Who knows . . . has Heaven come
At last to save me?)

(Forse . . . del ciel l'aita
A me soccorre.)

CARLOS

I'll take his life!

Colui morrà!

CHORUS
(*to Carlos who struggles to free himself*)

Quiet!

Vieni.

CARLOS
(*to Don Alvaro*)

Behold the man who killed my father!

Carnefice del padre mio!

(*The patrol drags him off.*)

ALVARO
(*throwing down his sword*)

What hope is left me? O God of mercy
Oh hear me, come to inspire me . . .
A cloister, a hermitage, some holy altar
May bring me the peace my heart yearns to find.

Or che mi resta! Pietoso Iddio,
Tu ispira, illumina il mio pensier.
Al chiostro, all'eremo, ai santi altari
L'oblio, la pace chiegga il guerrier.

(*He leaves.*)

---

* The 1862 version continued at this point with Alvaro's *Scena and Aria Finale Three*, which ended the whole Act. See page 97.

Scene Ten. *Sunrise: drum-roll and trumpet calls announce reveille. The stage gradually fills: Spanish and Italian soldiers of all ranks come out of the tents, collecting muskets, swords, buckling uniforms, etc. . . . . Drummer boys play at dice on their drums. Vivandières sell drinks, fruit, bread, etc.. Preziosilla, in her caravan, tells fortunes – the whole scene is very lively. / No. 23 Chorus and Couplets*

CHORUS

Drums and fifes are loudly sounding,	Lorche pifferi e tamburi
Music sounds in praise of fighting,	Par che assordino la terra
War's delightful, war's exciting,	Siam felici, ch'è la guerra
Joyful music calls us today.	Gioia, vita al militar.
Army life is all adventure,	Vita gaia, avventurosa,
Welcome joy and banish sorrow,	Cui non cal doman nè ieri,
Here today and gone tomorrow,	Ch'ama tutti i suoi pensieri
Gather rosebuds while we may.	Sol nell'oggi concentrar.

PREZIOSILLA
(*to the girls*)

Step up, my pretty maidens,	Venite all'indovina
For I have news to sell you,	Ch'è giunta di lontano,
And I alone call tell you	E puote a voi l'arcano
What fortune holds for you.	Futuro decifrar.

(*to the soldiers*)

Step up, my brave young soldiers,	Correte a lei d'intorno,
And you will soon discover,	La mano le porgete,
If there's a rival lover	Le amanti apprenderete
Or if your girl is true.	Se fide vi restar.

CHORUS

Consult the fortune-teller,	Andate all'indovina
And you will soon discover,	La mano le porgiamo,
If there's a rival lover,	Le belle udir possiamo
Or if your girl is true.	Se fide a noi restar.

PREZIOSILLA

If you would go to Heaven,	Chi vuole il paradiso
Then be a brave crusader,	S'accenda di valore,
Defeat the fierce invader,	E il barbaro invasore
And send him on his way.	S'accinga a discacciar.
Consult the fortune teller,	Avanti, avanti, avanti,
The stars are in your favour,	Predirvi sentirete
My words will make you braver,	Qual premio coglierete
I'll bring you luck today.	Dal vostro battagliar.

CHORUS

Consult the fortune-teller,	Avanti, avanti, avanti,
The stars are in your favour,	Predirci sentiremo
Her words will make you braver,	Qual premio coglieremo
She'll bring us luck today.	Dal nostro battagliar.

They gather around her. / No. 24 Scena and Arietta

SOLDIERS
(*The vivandières pour out drinks for the soldiers.*)

Hey, vivandières, we're thirsty!	Qua, vivandiere, un sorso.

1st SOLDIER

Long life to all brave soldiers!	Alla salute nostra!

ALL
(*drinking*)

Viva!   Viva!

2nd SOLDIER

To Spain –   A Spagna!

And Italy united!	Ed all'Italia unite!

92

Evviva!   Evviva!

PREZIOSILLA

I toast our leader,   Al nostro eroe
Don Federico Herreros.   Don Federico Herreros.

ALL

Viva! Viva!   Viva! Viva!

1st SOLDIER

Here's to his brave companion,   Ed al suo degno amico,
Don Felice de Bornos.   Don Felice de Bornos.

ALL

Viva! Viva!   Viva! Viva!

Scene Eleven. *The attention turns to the pedlar Trabuco, who comes from a stall on the left with a tray round his neck on which are various objects of small value.*

TRABUCO

Who wants to buy things, I sell them cheaply,   A buon mercato chi vuol comprare
Razors, brooches, soap sweetly perfumed.   Forbici, spille, sapon perfetto.
                                                 (*They surround him.*)
Who wants to sell things, I pay good money,   Io vendo e compro qualunque oggetto,
You'll get a bargain, and I pay cash.   Concludo a pronti qualunque affare.

1st SOLDIER
(*showing something*)

I've got a ring here, what will you pay?   Ho qui un monile, quanto mi dai?

2nd SOLDIER
(*showing something*)

And here's a necklace. For cash, I'll sell it.   Ve' una collana? Se vuoi, la vendo.

3rd SOLDIER
(*showing something*)

I have some earrings, what will you pay?   Questi orecchini li pagherai?

CHORUS
(*showing watches, rings, etc.*)

We want to sell to you ...   Vogliamo vendere ...

TRABUCO

All junk you show me!   Ma quanto vedo
Not worth the taking, cheap imitation.   Tutto è robaccia, brutta robaccia.

CHORUS

Thief of a pedlar, go to damnation!   Tale, o furfante, è la tua faccia.

TRABUCO

But let me price it, let me value it ... for   Pure aggiustiamoci ... per ogni pezzo
  every piece
I'll give thirty soldi ...   Do trenta soldi.

ALL
(*in an uproar*)

He wants to rob us!   Da ladro è il prezzo.

TRABUCO

Don't get excited ... Because I'm generous,   Ih, quanta furia! ... C'intenderemo,
I'll make it forty, I'll make it forty ...   Qualch'altro soldo v'aggiungeremo ...
Give me the merchandise!   Date qua, subito ...

CHORUS

Show us your money,
First let us see it, show us your money.

Purchè all'istante
Venga il denaro bello e sonante.

TRABUCO

First hand it over ... Come, you can
trust me.

Prima la merce ... qua ... colle buone.

SOLDIERS
(handing over the goods)

My ring.

A te.

OTHERS
(handing over more goods)

For this?

A te.

OTHERS
(handing over even more)

For this?

A te.

TRABUCO
(taking them, paying for each)

Take that, take that ... I'm going!

A voi, a voi, benone!

CHORUS
(chasing him off)

And now be off with you!

Al diavol vattene ...

TRABUCO
(aside, contented)

(I've done good business here today!)

(Che buon affar!)

(going off to sell elsewhere)

Who wants to buy things? Who wants to
sell things ...

A buon mercato chi vuol comprar ...

Scene Twelve. *Enter a group of begging peasants with their children. / No. 25 Chorus*

PEASANTS

Give us bread for Heaven's sake;
By this war our farms were wasted,
Three long days no food we've tasted,
We are starving, give us bread.

Pane, pan, per carità;
Tetti e campi devastati
N'ha la guerra, ed affamati
Cerchiam pane per pietà.

Scene Thirteen. *The same, and some recruits, who arrive weeping, under escort.*

RECRUITS

Torn from the arms of our sorrowful
mothers,
Seized by the army, to battles we roam.
Taken away from our sisters and brothers,
We are unhappy and want to go home.

Povere madri deserte nel pianto
Per dura forza dovemmo lasciar.
Della beltà n'han rapiti all'incanto,
A nostre case vogliamo tornar.

VIVANDIÈRES
(gaily accosting the recruits and offering them drinks)

Dry those tears, you brave young fellows,
No more crying for your mothers,
We shall love you as our brothers,
We can cheer you in our arms.

Non piangete, giovinotti,
Per le madri e per le belle;
V'ameremo quai sorelle,
Vi sapremo consolar.

Don't be frightened, we'll not harm you;
Dry your tears and stop your crying,
No more weeping, no more sighing,
No more thinking of the past.

Certo il diavolo non siamo;
Quelle lacrime tergete,
Al passato, ben vedrete,
Ora è inutile pensar.

(taking one or two by the arm, joking and reproachful)

How disgraceful! Oh how shocking!	Che vergogna! . . . su, coraggio . . .
Little babies need a rocking?	Bei figliuoli, siete pazzi
If our soldiers see you crying	Se piangete quai ragazzi
You will never live it down.	Vi farete corbellar.
Look around and see these ladies,	Un'occhiata a voi d'intorno,
See their lovely smiling faces;	E scommetto che indovino;
Calm your fears in their embraces,	Ci sarà più d'un visino
Dry your eyes, and dry them fast.	Che sapravvi consolar.

No. 26 Chorus and Tarantella

The vivandières, without restraint, take the recruits by the arm and begin a very lively general dance. Soon the confusion and revelry are at their height.

ALL

Viva, viva, dance invites us,	Nella guerra è la follia
In the army love unites us,	Che dee il campo rallegrar;
Viva, viva, all excites us	Viva, viva, la pazzia,
And dance invites us to sport and play!	Che qui sola ha da regnar!

Scene Fourteen. *Melitone enters and is whirled into the vortex of the dance . . . for a moment he is compelled to spin round with the Vivandières. He manages at last to stop, and cries out: / No. 27 Sermon*

MELITONE
(severely)

Fie, fie! . . . Shame on you all! Disgraceful creatures!	Toh, toh! . . . Poffare il mondo! o che tempone.
So your fun's just beginning! In time I caught you!	Corre ben l'avventura! . . . Anch'io ci sono!
I left my cloister to *medicate* the wounded [21]	Venni di Spagna a *medicar* ferite
And *mendicate* their souls. What find I? Is this	Ed alme a *mendicar*. Che vedo! è questo
A camp of Christian soldiers, or are you pagans,	Un campo di Cristiani, o siete Turchi?
Turkish barbarians, Turkish barbarians?	Siete Turchi, siete Turchi, o siete Turchi?
Whoever saw the Sabbath day profaned	Dove s'è visto a berteggiar la santa
By dancing and drink? You're more successful	Domenica così? . . . Ben più faccenda
With your *bottles* of wine than with your *battles*!	Le *bottiglie* vi dan che le *battaglie*!
Instead of putting on sackcloth and ashes	E invece di vestir *cenere e sacco*,
You're consorting with Venus and with Bacchus?	Qui si tresca con *Venere* e con *Bacco*?
The world's a sad place of weeping and sighing;	Il mondo è fatto una casa di pianto;
Now every *priesthouse*	Ogni *convento*
Is changed into a *feasthouse*! Now every *storehouse*	Or è *covo* del *vento*! I *Santuari*
Of wisdom and grace becomes a *whorehouse*!	Spelonche diventar di *sanguinari*;
Each Sanctuary of holy institution	Perfino i *tabernacoli di Cristo*
Has become a house of prostitution.	Fatti son *recettacoli del tristo*.
All the world's topsy-turvy . . . I'll tell you why: *Pro peccata vestra*	Tutto è a soqquadro . . . e la ragion? . . . pro peccata vestra
Your sins stink and fester . . .	Pei vestri peccati.

ITALIAN SOLDIERS

Enough, good friar!	Ah frate . . . frate!

MELITONE

You are all of you	Voi le feste
Deceivers, blasphemers, unbelievers . . .	Calpestate, rubate, bestemmiate . . .

ITALIAN SOLDIERS

You fat old scoundrel! . . .	Togone infame! . . .

Keep it up, keep preaching!   Segui pur, padruccio.

MELITONE

From top to toe you wallow in your vileness . . .	E membra e capi siete d'una stampa . . .
You're all heretics . . .	Tutti eretici . . .
You are all of you sinks of profanation.	Tutti, tutti cloaca di peccati,
You have foregone all chance of your salvation,	E finchè il mondo puzzi di tal *pece*.
There's no hope of your country's liberation . . .	Non isperi la terra alcuna *pace*.

ITALIAN SOLDIERS
(mobbing him)

Let him have it . . .   Dalli, dalli . . .

SPANISH SOLDIERS
(protecting him)

We'll defend you . . .   Scappa, scappa . . .

MELITONE
(The Italian soldiers try to man-handle him, but he escapes, still preaching vigorously.)

You are heading for damnation . . .   Con tal *pece* non v'è *pace* . . .

No. 28 Rataplan

PREZIOSILLA
(to the soldiers following Melitone as he leaves the stage)

Oh, leave him to his preaching . . .	Lasciatelo, ch'ei vada . . .
Attacking a holy friar! How disgraceful!	Far guerra ad un cappuccio! . . . bella impresa! . . .
Not listening? Then let the drum defend and save him!	Non m'odon? . . . sia il tamburo sua difesa.

(She picks up a small drum at random and, imitated by several drummer boys, begins to play it. Soldiers surround her, followed by all the camp followers, etc., who swarm back onto the stage.)

Rataplan, rataplan, on to glory,	[23] Rataplan, rataplan, della gloria
Drums are beating and bugles reply;	Nel soldato ritempra l'ardor;
Rataplan, rataplan, on to glory,	Rataplan, rataplan, di vittoria
Hear them call you to conquer or die!	Questo suono è segnal precursor!
Rataplan, rataplan, we assemble,	Rataplan, rataplan, or le schiere
See the banners of victory held high!	Son guidate, raccolte a pugnar!
Rataplan, rataplan, how they tremble!	Rataplan, rataplan, le bandiere
When we march every foeman will fly!	Del nemico si veggon piegar!
Rataplan, pim, pum, pum . . . to the rolling	Rataplan, pim, pum, pum, inseguite
Beat march onward, pursue the flying foe!	Chi le terga, fuggendo, voltò . . .
When the heroes return in glory	Le gloriose ferite
Triumphant, every trumpet will blow!	Col trionfo il destin coronò.
Rataplan, on to glory!	Rataplan, rataplan, la vittoria!
On to victory with musket and sword!	Più rifulge de' figli al valor! . . .
Rataplan, rataplan, on to glory,	Rataplan, rataplan, la vittoria
Love and honour will be your reward.	Al guerriero conquista ogni cor.

(All run out. The curtain falls.)

End of the Act.

In the 1862 version, the Act continued with the Alvaro-Carlos duet, Scene Eight above (Scene Eleven in the 1862 version). At the close of the duet, the Act ended with this Scene Twelve, Alvaro's 'Scena and Aria Finale', which Verdi dropped in 1869 altogether.

Act Three. Scene Twelve. *A fight is heard, and then Don Alvaro returns to the stage in the greatest agitation. / Scena and Aria Finale Three.*

ALVARO

And I have killed him! Oh horror!	Qual sangue sparsi! Orrore!
An icy hand has seized on my heart!	Il cor mi stringe ferreaman!
I have slain him, though I loved him.	Io l'uccisi, e l'amava!
Yet he meant to take your life, Leonora!	Qual t'attende fiero colpo, Leonora!
A sea of blood now divides us for ever!	Un mar di sangue or ne divido per sempre!
For he was my friend, he was my brother!	Ei m'era fratel, m'era fratello!
I killed him. Alas!	L'uccisi! Ohimè!
An angel with a fiery sword of vengeance	L'angiol di Dio con ignea spada
Pursues me, inspires me, destroys me!	M'insegue, m'incalza, atterra!
Ah! The mark of Cain is branded on my forehead,	Ah! come Caino son maledetto in terra,
I am accursed.	Son maledetto.
Oh have mercy on me, forgive O Lord,	Miserere di me, pietà, Signor,
Forgive me for the wrongs I've done.	Concedi il tuo perdon a tanto errore.

GRENADIERS
(entering from left)

To arms! Germans are advancing.	All' armi! Ecco i Tedeschi!

(Twelve choristers enter from the left.)

See where tents are blazing,	Arde la regal tenda,
So lead us to the fight.	Venite, capitan.
To death or glory!	Vittoria, o morte.

(Exeunt running to the right.)

ALVARO

May death come to claim me,	S'affronti la morte,
And end my sad existence!	E alfin sia compita
May death come to claim me	Di questa mia vita
And end my useless life.	La barbara sorte.
To death or glory.	Si voli a morte.
Ah! If destiny decides	Ah! e se ancora il fato
To prolong my weary days,	Mi danni a soffrir,
To God I'll consecrate them,	A Dio consacrarlo
And die in a cloister.	Io giuro morire.
Away, to die!	Andiam, andiam.

(He runs out following the Grenadiers.)

End of the Act.

Act Four

In the neighbourhood of Hornachuelos

Scene One. *A courtyard inside the monastery of Our Lady of the Angels. A shabby colonnade around a small cloister with orange trees, oleanders and jasmine. To the left, the main door to the road: to the right, another with a sign 'Cloister'. Father Guardiano paces up and down reading his breviary. A crowd of beggars of all ages push in from the main door where they have been waiting, and shout outside the other. They have rough bowls, pipkins or platters in their hands. / No. 29 Chorus and Aria Buffa*

CHORUS

Food, for love of God!	Fate la carità.
An hour we've had to wait here!	È un ora che aspettiamo!
There's no one at the gate here,	Andarcene dobbiamo,
We'll have to go away.	Fate la carità.

Scene Two. *Melitone, his stomach covered with a large white apron, comes from the right, and, helped by another lay-brother, carries a large two-handled cauldron, which they set down centre stage; the lay-brother departs.*

MELITONE
(beginning to serve the soup with a ladle)

Hey! You're not in an alehouse! . . . Quiet! . . .	Che? Siete all'osteria? . . . Quieti . . .

WOMEN
(jostling)

Give some to me.	Qui, presto a me.

OLD MEN

You've got a larger portion!	Quante porzioni a loro!

OTHER BEGGARS

You're trying to take it all.	Tutti vorrian per sè.

ALL

Three is enough for Mary! . . .	N'ebbe già tre Maria!

BEGGAR WOMAN
(to Melitone)

Give me four	Quattro a me . . .

ALL

You want four!	Quattro a lei!

THE SAME BEGGAR WOMAN

Yes, because I have six children . . .	Si, perchè ho sei figlioli . . .

MELITONE

And why do you have six?	Perchè ne avete sei?

THE SAME BEGGAR WOMAN

Because the Good Lord sent them . . .	Perchè li mandò Iddio . . .

MELITONE

The Good Lord sent them . . . You'd not have them	Sì, sì, Dio . . . Non li avreste
If you, like me, were holy, avoiding temptation	Se al par di me voi pure la schiena percoteste
With penance meek and lowly: so spend your nights as I do,	Con aspra disciplina, e più le notti intere
Reciting your Hail Marys and many Misereres . . .	Passaste recitando rosari e Miserere . . .

GUARDIANO

My son . . .   Fratel . . .

MELITONE

But it's revolting, they've children by the   Ma tai pezzenti son di fecondità
score,
These people breed like rabbits . . .   Davvero spaventosa.

GUARDIANO

Be patient with the poor.   Abbiate carità.

OLD MEN

So ladle out those scrapings and let's have [24]   Un po' di quel fondaccio ancora ne donate.
fair dividing.

MELITONE

You dare to call this scrapings, the food the   Il ben di Dio, bricconi, fondaccio voi
Lord's providing?   chiamate?

BEGGARS
(offering their bowls again)

Well give some to me . . . and me . . .   A me, padre . . . A me . . .

MELITONE

I'm sick of all your whining,   Oh, andatene in malora,
A whacking with my ladle will interrupt   O il ramaiol sul capo v'aggiusto ben or
your dining . . .   ora . . .
I'm running out of patience!   Io perdo la pazienza!

GUARDIANO

Oh be kind . . .   Carità . . .

WOMEN

Yes, we were treated kindly by Father   Più carità ne usava il Padre Raffaello.
Raffael.

MELITONE

Yes, for one week he lasted, and then he   Sì, sì, ma in otto giorni, avutone abbastanza.
was defeated.
Worn out by all your whining, to a cell he   Di poveri e minestra, restò nella sua stanza,
soon retreated,
So now it is the duty of poor old Melitone   E scaricò la soma sul dosso a Melitone . . .
To wield this heavy ladle and serve your   E poi con tal canaglia usar dovrò le buone?
minestrone.

GUARDIANO

Succour the poor and suffering . . . recall   Soffrono tanto i poveri . . . la carità è un
our good Lord's lesson.   dovere.

MELITONE

Succour these? They're not suffering, and   Carità con costoro che il fanno per
begging's their profession!   mestiere?
If our great bell appealed to them they'd   Che un campanile abbattere co' pugni
steal it from the steeple;   sarien buoni,
They said my stew was scrapings, too well I   Che dicono fondaccio il ben di Dio . . .
know these people . . . You rabble!   Bricconi!

WOMEN

Good Father Raffaele! . . .   Oh, il Padre Raffaele . . .

OTHER BEGGARS

Was a holy man! An angel!   Era un angelo! Un santo!

MELITONE

Hoping that you'll provoke me!   Non m'annoiate tanto!
(He hurriedly finishes serving.)

99

So take what's left and eat it up, I'm tired of all your chatter ...	Il resto a voi, prendetevi, – non voglio più parole ...

(He kicks over the cauldron.)

Take what is left, and scoop it up, and then be on your way.	Fuori di qua, lasciatemi, – si, fuori, al sole, al sole;
You beggars worse than Lazarus, harpies and beasts of prey,	Pezzenti più di Lazzaro – sacchi di pravità.
Be off, be off, to hell with you, you get no more today.	Via, via, bricconi, al diavolo, – toglietevi di qua.

(In a rage, he chases them away in confusion, flapping at them with his apron, which he has taken off. He closes the door on them, remaining extremely cross and tired.)

Scene Three. *Father Guardiano and Brother Melitone. / No. 30 Scena and Duet*

MELITONE
(wiping the sweat from his brow with a white handkerchief, which he takes from his sleeve)

Oof! ... My patience is quite exhausted!	Auf! ... Pazienza non v'ha che basti!

GUARDIANO

Heaven	Troppa
Did not grant you much patience.	Dal Signor non ne aveste.
To feed the suffering poor in their need is a duty	Facendo carità un dover s'adempie
That angels would delight in!	Da render fiero un angiol!

MELITONE
(taking snuff)

After three days	Che al mio posto
In my job an angel	In tre dì finirebbe
Would serve them *blows* for supper ...	Col *minestar* de' schiaffi ...

GUARDIANO

Be silent; be humble, Meliton, you must not	Tacete; umil sia Meliton, nè soffrà
Be jealous if they favour Raffaele.	Se veda preferirsi Raffaele.

MELITONE

Jealous? No ... I'm fond of the man, but, he's so mysterious ...	Io? ... No ... amico gli son, ma ha certi gesti ...
Talks to himself, acts so strangely ...	Parla da sè ... ha cert'occhi ...

GUARDIANO

That's from praying	Son le preci,
And fasting ...	Il digiun ...

MELITONE

He was working in the garden,	Ier nell'orto lavorava
His eyes were wildly rolling, jokingly I	Cotanto stralunato, che scherzando
Told him: 'You're like a dark	Dissi: 'Padre ... un mulatto
Mulatto ...' He looked so angry	Parmi ...' Guardommi bieco,
I thought he'd strike me, and ...	Strinse le pugna, e ...

GUARDIANO

Continue ...	Ebbene?

MELITONE

Then a bright	... quando cadde
Flash of lightning struck the belfry tower, and he rushed	Sul campanil la folgore, ed usciva
Through the howling tempest. I called out: 'You're like a	Fra la tempesta, gli gridai: 'Mi sembra
Savage Indian ...' His yell froze	Indian selvaggio ...' Un urlo
My bones to the very marrow.	Cacciò che mi gelava.

GUARDIANO

What else was said?	Che v'ha a ridir?

MELITONE

Nothing, but I remembered	Nulla, ma il guardo e penso.
Your story, that the devil	Narraste che il demonio
Once came to live here disguised as a friar . . .	Qui stette un tempo un abito da frate . . .
Could Father Raffaele be his relation?	Gli fosse il Padre Raffael parente?

GUARDIANO

You're jumping to conclusions . . . the tale is true . . .	Giudizi temerari . . . il ver narrari . . .
But only my Superior really knew	Ma n'ebbe il Superior rivelazione
The details . . . Not I.	Allora . . . Io, no.

MELITONE

So it is true!	Ciò è vero!
But Raffael's a strange one! What's the reason?	Ma strano è molto il Padre! . . . La ragione?

GUARDIANO

The world and life's delusions,	[24] Del mondo i disinganni,
His penance everlasting,	L'assidua penitenza,
His vigils, and his fasting	Le veglie, l'astinenza
Confuse his troubled brain.	Quell'anima turbar.

MELITONE

The world and its delusions,	[24] Saranno i disinganni,
His penance everlasting,	L'assidua penitenza,
His vigils and his fasting	Le veglie, l'astinenza
Have driven him insane!	Che il capo gli guastar!

The bell at the door is rung violently. / No. 31 Scena

GUARDIANO

See who is there . . . admit him . . .	Giunge qualcun . . . aprite . . .

(*He leaves.*)

Scene Four. *Brother Melitone; Don Carlos, who is wearing a large cloak, makes a bold entrance.*

CARLOS
(*sharply*)

Are you the porter?	Siete voi il portiere?

MELITONE

(The man must be a blockhead!)	(È goffo ben costui!)
I opened, therefore . . .	Se apersi, parmi . . .

CARLOS

Where's Father Raffaele?	Il Padre Raffaele?

MELITONE

(Another!) We've two of that name;	(Un altro!) Due ne abbiamo . . .
One's from Porcuna, portly,	L'un di Porcuna, grasso,
Deaf as a mole, poor fellow, the other's scrawny,	Sordo come una talpa, un altro arno,
Swarthy, wild-eyed . . . (Heavens, what wild eyes!) Which is your man?	Bruno, occhi . . . (Ciel, quali occhi!) voi chiedete?

CARLOS

The one from Hades.	Quel dell'inferno.

MELITONE

(I knew it . . .) Who wants to see him?	(È desso . . .) E chi gli annuncio?

CARLOS

What's that to you . . .	Un cavalier . . .

MELITONE

(Such manners! No education!)   (Qual boria! è un mal arnese.)

(*He leaves.*)

Scene Five.* *Don Carlos, later Don Alvaro in a monk's habit. / No. 32 Scena*

CARLOS

In vain, Alvaro, have you tried to flee me,	Invano Alvaro ti celasti al mondo
And the cloak of religion	E d'ipocrita veste
No longer serves you for disguise.	Scudo facesti alla viltà. Del chiostro
Though hiding in a cloister, I have come to find you,	Ove t'ascondi m'additar la via
Led by my burning thirst for vengeance; and this time	L'odio e la sete di vendetta; alcuno
No friendly troops will come to save you; your blood,	Qui non sarà che ne divida; il sangue,
Your blood alone can erase the crime	Solo il tuo sangue può lavar l'oltraggio
That has long stained my honour:	Che machiò l'onor mio:
Today that blood will flow, by God I swear it.	E tutto il verserò, lo giuro a Dio.

ALVARO

My brother . . .   Fratello . . .

CARLOS

You remember me!   Riconoscimi.

ALVARO

Don Carlos! You! Still living!   Don Carlo! Voi vivente!

CARLOS

For five long years I sought you.	Da un lustro ne vo in traccia,
And now at last I find where you are hiding . . .	Ti trovo finalmente . . .
Your blood alone can pay the price†	[25] Col sangue sol cancellasi
Of crime and vile dishonour.	L'infamia ed il delitto,
My hand alone will shed that blood:	Ch'io ti punisca è scritto
By Fate it is decreed.	Sul libro del destin.
You, once a soldier, now play the monk,	Tu prode fosti, or monaco,
No weapon at your side . . .	Un'arma qui non hai . . .
Since I have sworn to take your life,	Deggio il tuo sangue spargere;
Choose one; you or I must die . . .	Scegli, due ne portai . . .

ALVARO

I was a soldier . . . I grant you;	Vissi nel mondo . . . intendo;
Now let my garments speak for me,	Or queste vesti . . . l'eremo
Tell you that I'm repentant,	Dicon che i falli ammendo,
I give my life to God.	Che penitente è il cor.
Depart in peace.	Lasciatemi!

---

* In 1862 this recitative was briefer:

Scene Five. */ No. 33 Scena and Duet*

CARLOS

You thought me dead, Alvaro, but fate has spared me . . .	Spento mi credi, Alvaro, ma ancor vivo
My hour of vengeance is delayed no longer.	Nè di vendetta più l'onor fia privo.

† In 1862, this and the next three lines were:

Though in our duel I fell to you,	Se caddi un giorno esanime
Though you believed you'd slain me,	Dalla tua man trafitto,
God, who had seen your base crime,	Dio d'ogni tuo delitto
Saved me to fight again.	Serbommi punitor.

CARLOS

The cloister and	Difendere
The cassock will not save you,	Quel saio, nè il deserto
You coward, you must answer me ...	Codardo, te non possono ...

ALVARO
(He starts back in amazement.)

A coward! You'll regret that ...	Codardo! Tale asserto ...

(controlling himself, aside)

(No! Oh, help me now, my Saviour!)	(No! ... assistimi, Signor!)

(to Don Carlos)

[26] Le minaccie, i fieri accenti	
All your fiery threats of vengeance,	[26] Le minaccie, i fieri accenti
Cannot turn me from repentance,	Portin seco in preda i venti,
Let us now be reconciled,	Perdonatemi ... pietà,
O my friend, forgive, forgive.	O fratel, pietà, pietà.

Let my mild words disarm you,	A che offendere cotanto
For I never sought to harm you ...	Chi fu solo sventurato?
It was fate that killed your father,	Deh, chiniam la fronte al fato,
My friend, forgive, forgive.	O fratel, pietà, pietà.

CARLOS

You defile the name of friendship ...	Tu contamini tal nome ...
Ah! Of my sister you have robbed me,	Una suora mi lasciasti
You abandoned and betrayed her,	Che tradita abbandonasti,
And left her to her shame.	All'infamia, al disonor.

ALVARO

It's untrue, I did not wrong her,	No, non fu disonorata,
Let me swear it in sight of Heaven;	Ve lo giura un sacerdote:
Here on earth I once adored her	Sulla terra l'ho adorata
With a chaste and pure devotion.	Come in cielo amar si puote ...
I am true and if she loves me	L'amo ancora, e s'ella m'ama
That is all I ask of life.	Più non brama questo cor.

CARLOS

Do not try to calm my fury	Non si placa il mio furore
By your lies and vile pretending.	Per mendace e vile accento.
Choose a sword and come to fight me,	L'arme impugna, ed al cimento
I'll avenge my father's life.	Scendi meco, o traditor.

ALVARO

If my words and my repentance	Se i rimorsi, il pianto omai
Cannot show you what I feel,	Non vi parlano per me,
Though to man I've never knelt,	Qual nessun mi vide mai,
At your feet I humbly kneel.	Io mi prostro al vostro piè.

(He kneels.)

CARLOS

Ah! The baseness of your lineage	Ah, la macchia del tuo stemma
Now is proved by your behaviour.	Or provasti con quest'atto!

ALVARO
(springing to his feet in sudden fury)

No, my race is high and noble ...	Desso splende più che gemma ...

CARLOS

Tainted blood of a mulatto!	Sangue il tinge di mulatto.

ALVARO
(no longer able to curb his fury)

You shall pay for that, you liar.	Per la gola voi mentite ...
Give me a weapon ...	A me un brando ...

(He seizes a sword.)

A weapon ... obey me.	Un brando ... Uscite.
A sword ends your lying ... Lead on now!	Un brando, un brando ... Uscite!

103

So you'll fight me?   Finalmente! . . .
                          (*moving away*)

ALVARO
(*recovering himself*)

    No . . . for Satan   No . . . l'inferno
Shall not triumph . . . Go, go quickly . . .   Non trionfi . . . Va' riparti . . .

(*He throws down the sword.*)

CARLOS

So you still intend to cheat me?   Ti fai dunque di me scherno?
If you still refuse to face me,   S'ora meco misurati,
Then I brand you as a coward,   O vigliacco, non hai core,
And I mark you for dishonour . . .   Ti consacro al disonore . . .

(*He strikes him on the face.*)

ALVARO
(*furiously*)

Ah! That insult seals your sentence!   Ah, segnasti la tua sorte!
(*seizing the sword again*)

CARLOS

Vengeance . . . no more repentance.   Morte . . . a entrambi morte.

BOTH

Vengeance . . . death awaits you today . . .   Morte . . . vieni, vieni a morte,
To death, away!   A morte andiam.

(*They rush off left.*)

Scene Six. *A mountain gorge between precipitous rocks, through which runs a little stream. Towards the back a cave with a door and above it, a bell, the bell-rope within. It is sunset, growing slowly darker; later, brilliant moonlight. Leonora, pale and careworn, comes out of the cave in distress.* / *Melodia No. 33* [1]

LEONORA
(*At first from within the cave, then she appears on the threshold.*)

Father, Father, Father in Heaven, grant [27]   Pace, pace, mio Dio; pace mio Dio!
  me peace of mind!
Cruel misfortune   Cruda sventura
Has doomed my life to grief.   M'astringe, ahimè, a languir;
Every day I suffer, every day I suffer   Come il dì primo da tant' anni dura
And never find relief.   Profondo il mio soffrir.
I loved, 'tis true! . . . but You, O God,   L'amai, gli è ver! . . . ma di beltà e valore
  endowed him
With every grace and charm . . .   Cotanto Iddio l'ornò
I love him still, ah how could I forget him   Che l'amo ancor, nè togliermi dal core
Or tear him from my heart?   L'immagin sua saprò.
A cruel fate! . . . A cruel fate! We were   Fatalità! . . . fatalità! . . . un delitto
  parted,
Were parted by a crime!   Disgiunti n'ha quaggiù! . . .
Alvaro, I love you, and yet in Heaven 'tis   Alvaro, io t'amo, e su nel cielo è scritto:
  fated:
We'll never meet again!   Non ti vedrò mai più!
O Father, Father, let me die now; death   Oh Dio, Dio, fa ch'io muoia: chè la calma
Alone can bring release.   Può darmi morte sol.
In vain for pardon in my bitter sorrow,   Invan la pace qui sperò quest'alma
My bitter sorrow, I yearn in vain.   In preda a tanto duol.
        (*crossing to a large stone on which Father Guardiano has left some food for her*)
This food they bring me prolongs my sad   Misero pane . . . a prolungarmi vieni
  existence
When I would rather perish . . . Who   La sconsolata vita . . . Ma chi giunge?
  approaches?

104

Who dares profane this place of holy refuge?	Chi profanare ardisce il sacro loco?
He is accursed! He is accursed!	Maledizione! . . . Maledizione! . . .

(Returning quickly to the cave, she shuts herself in.)

The 1869 ending

Scene Seven. *The clash of swords is heard off-stage. / No. 34 Scena and Final Terzetto*

CARLOS
(off-stage)

I'm dying . . . Hear my confession! . . .	Io muoio! . . . Confessione! . . . l'alma salvate.
Save me from damnation.	

ALVARO
(appearing on-stage with a blood-stained sword)

Again I shed the blood of a Vargas . . .	È questo ancor sangue d'un Vargas . . .

CARLOS
(still off-stage)

Hear my confession . . .	Confessione . . .

ALVARO
(He throws away his sword.)

There's a curse upon me: but close by	Maledetto io son; ma è presso
There lives a holy hermit.	Un eremita.

(He runs to the cave and knocks on the door.)

Come forth to shrive a man	A confortar correte
At point of death.	Un uom che muor . . .

LEONORA
(within)

I dare not.	Nol posso.

ALVARO

My brother! In God's most holy name . . .	Fratello! In nome del Signor . . .

LEONORA

I dare not.	Nol posso.

ALVARO

He's dying!	E d'uopo!

(knocking louder)

LEONORA

Oh help me! Oh help me!	Aiuto! Auito!

(ringing the bell from within)

ALVARO

He is dying.	Deh, venite!

Scene Eight. *Leonora appears at the entrance.*

LEONORA

Rash intruder! By Heaven you are accursed!	Temerari, del ciel l'ira fuggite!

ALVARO

It's a woman! It's her voice! . . . Ah no . . . a	Una donna! qual voce . . . ah no . . . uno
delusion . . .	spettro . . .

LEONORA
(recognising Don Alvaro)

Oh Heaven!	Che miro?

105

You ... Leonora ...   Tu ... Leonora ...

LEONORA

It is Alvaro ...   Egli è ben desso ...
(advancing towards him)
Ah, once again I see you ...   Io ti riveggo ancora ...

ALVARO

Leave me ... Do not approach ...   Lungi ... lungi da me ... queste mie mani
  My hands are
Stained with blood of the dying. Avoid me!   Grondano sangue ... Indietro!

LEONORA

Ah, what say you?   Che mai parli?

ALVARO
(pointing)

There lies a dying man ...   Là giace spento un uom ...

LEONORA

And did you kill him?   Tu l'uccidesti?

ALVARO

I struggled vainly to avoid this duel.   Tutto tentai per evitar la pugna.
I'd left the world behind me.   Chiusi i miei dì nel chiostro.
He came to find me ... made me fight ... Ei mi raggiunse ... m'insultò ... l'uccisi ...
  I've killed him ...

LEONORA

Who is he?   Ed era?

ALVARO

He's Don Carlos!   Tuo fratello!

LEONORA

My brother!   Gran Dio!

(She runs to where Carlos is lying in the wood.)

ALVARO

O cruel destiny!   Destino avverso,
Once again you deride me! ...   Come a scherno mi prendi!
My Leonora lives, and I live to find her, Vive Leonora e ritrovarla deggio
But on the day when her brother's blood is   Or che versai di suo fratello il sangue!
  fresh upon me.

LEONORA
(crying out)

Ah!   Ah!

ALVARO

A cry ... What happened?   Qual grido! ... che avvene?

Scene Eleven. *Leonora, mortally wounded, staggers forward supported by Father Guardiano.*

ALVARO

Heavens! She's wounded?   Ella ... ferita! ...

LEONORA
(dying)

In hour of dying, he could not forgive   Nell'ora estrema perdonar non seppe ...
  me ...
And with my life I pay for his dishonour.   E l'onta vendicò nel sangue mio.

ALVARO
(savagely)

Can we never escape
From the vengeance of Heaven! . . . May
  God be cursed!

E tu paga non eri
O vendetta di Dio! . . . Maledizione!

GUARDIANO
(solemnly)

Do not blaspheme but kneel and pray.
God is both righteous and He is holy.
He can lead to joys unfading
After this life of sorrow . . .
Cease from your words of rage and sacrilege,
Offer a prayer for pardon.
See this angel flying
Toward the throne of God . . .

[29] Non imprecare; umiliati
A Lui ch'è giusto e santo . . .
Che adduce a eterni gaudii
Per una vita di pianto . . .
D'ira e furor sacrilego
Non profferir parola,
Vedi quest'angiol vola
Al trono del Signor . . .

LEONORA
(in a faint voice)

Pray for his mercy . . .

Si, piangi . . . e prega.

ALVARO

    A criminal,
A man accursed by Heaven.
Oceans of blood divide us
Evermore.

    Un reprobo,
Un maledetto io sono.
Flutto di sangue innalzasi
Fra noi . . .

LEONORA

   I promise that Heaven
Will show you mercy.

    Di Dio il perdono
Io ti prometto . . .

GUARDIANO

   Penitence!

    Prostrati!

ALVARO

   Those tender accents . . .
How can I close my heart to them? . . .
Leonora, I am redeemed now.
(throwing himself on his knees at her feet)
By Heaven I am pardoned!

    A quell'accento
Più non poss'io resistere . . .
Leonora, io son redento,
Dal ciel son perdonato!

LEONORA AND GUARDIANO

O Lord, I thank Thee!

Sia lode a te, Signor.

LEONORA
(to Alvaro)

Gladly I go to wait for you
In that eternal country . . .
There where all strife is ended,
Where our love is blessed.

Lieta poss'io precederti
Alla promessa terra . . .
Là cesserà la guerra,
Santo l'amor sarà.

ALVARO

Am I condemned to linger on . . .
Alone on earth you leave me!
The guilty one alone lives on unpunished,
Though I alone transgressed.

Tu mi condanni a vivere,
E mi abbandoni intanto!
Il reo, io reo soltanto
Dunque impunito andrà!

GUARDIANO

Blessed by all her suffering
She will ascend to Heaven,
And her dying show the path
To peace and love.

Santa del suo martirio
Ella al Signore ascenda,
E il suo morir ne apprenda,
La fede e la pietà!

LEONORA

In Heaven, Alvaro, beloved,   In ciel t'attendo, addio!
I await you ... Alvaro ...   Ti precedo, Alvaro ...

(She dies.)

ALVARO

Dead now!   Morta!

GUARDIANO

Her soul's in Heaven.   Salita a Dio!

(Slow curtain.)

The End.

In 1862 the ending was different.

Scene Seven. *The sky is stormy. The stage slowly darkens. Don Alvaro and Don Carlos come down from a precipice on the right, running with their swords in their hands.*

ALVARO

Intruders in this place are held accursed, Chi preme questa terra è maledetto
But today we are both accursed!   Ma de'delitti è questo il giorno!
Here we'll duel! ...   Qui sostiamo! ...

(They fight furiously. Don Carlos is fatally wounded.)

CARLOS

I'm dying ... Hear my last confession, Io muoio! ... confession, mio Dio! l'alma
  hear my confession ...   salvate ...

ALVARO

(Again I shed the blood of a Vargas!)   È questo ancor sangue d'un Vargas! ...

CARLOS

Friar ... I confess ...   Padre ... Confession ...

ALVARO

There's a curse upon me;   Maledetto io son; ma è presso
But in there, there lives a hermit ...   Un eremita ...

CARLOS

Let him come to confess me ...   Per pietà ... affrettate.

ALVARO
(running to the cave, and knocking on the door)

Come out and shrive a man   A confortar correte
At point of death ...   Un uom che muor ...

LEONORA
(from within)

I dare not.   Nol posso.

ALVARO
(knocking with more urgency)

My brother ... in God's most holy name ... Fratello ... in nome del Signor ...

LEONORA

I dare not.   Nol posso.

ALVARO

He's dying.   È d'uopo!

LEONORA
(ringing the bell from within)

Oh help me! Oh help me! ...   Aiuto! Aiuto! ...

ALVARO

He is dying!   Deh, venite!

Scene Eight. *Leonora appears at the entrance.*

LEONORA

Rash intruder, by Heaven you are accursed!   Temerari, del ciel l'ira fuggite.

ALVARO
(coming down, overwhelmed with horror)

Oh Heaven! A woman! Her voice!   Oh cielo! una donna!... qual voce!
Leonora!   Leonora!

LEONORA

Alvaro! Don Alvaro!   Gran Dio! Don Alvaro!
(She comes down.)

LEONORA AND ALVARO

At last I see you near me, { Alvaro   Si dunque a me presso tu stavi, mio bene!
beloved!   { Leonora
This moment repays all my sad years of   Cancelli quest'ora d'un tempo le pene!
waiting!
You are beside me, my love!   Si a me presso, mio ben!

CARLOS

(So she was beside him all the time!)   (Ed erano insieme, ed erano insiem!)
My sister?   Sorella?

LEONORA

What hear I?   Chi sento?

CARLOS

You hear now the voice of the last   Del sangue tuo l'ultimo ti volge l'accento ...
Calatrava ...

LEONORA
(She embraces him.)

Don Carlos, my brother, ah let me   Don Carlo fratello, ti stringo al mio core ...
embrace you ...

CARLOS
(He stabs her in the breast.)

Ah! So I have my vengeance!   Ah! Or son vendicato!

(Don Carlos dies.)

ALVARO
(to Don Carlos)

What have you done? ... Oh horror!   Che festi tu? ... Orrore!

LEONORA

I forgive you my bro ...[ther]   Ti perdono fratel ...
Slain by the hand of destiny! ...   Vedi destin! ... io muoio! ...
Slain by the hand ... I'm dying!   Vedi destin! ... io muoio! ...
Alas, I leave you Alvaro,   Ahimè, ti lascio! Alvaro,
In Heaven we'll meet again, Alvaro ...   In ciel, ci rivedremo in ciel, Alvaro ...
Alvaro ... I love you ... we'll meet again   Alvaro ... io t'amo ... ci rivedrem in ciel ...
in Heaven ...

(Leonora dies.)

ALVARO

Leonora! My love, at last I find you! Ah!   Leonora! Alfine ti trovai! Si!
In death I find you!   Ti trovai morta!

(He remains motionless.)

Final Scene. *The thunder roars more than ever, there are more frequent flashes of lightning, and the friars are heard chanting the Miserere. At their approach, Don Álvaro turns around and runs up a rock on the left. Then Father Guardiano arrives, with the whole community bearing torches. They all stand amazed.*

MELITONE, GUARDIANO AND THE FRIARS

Miserere mei Deus, secundum magnum   Miserere mei Deus, secundum magnum
Misericordiam tuam miserere . . .   Misericordiam tuam miserere . . .

GUARDIANO

Great Heaven! Blood! Who's lying there?   Gran Dio! Sangue! Cadaveri!
The woman whom I sheltered! . . .   La donna penitente!

ALL

           It's a woman!   Una donna!
Slain there!   Cielo!

GUARDIANO

     Father Raffaele . . .   Padre Raffaele . . .

ALVARO

        You're mistaken,   Imbecille,
Here's no Father Raffaele . . .   Cerca il Padre Raffaele . . .
But a demon who was sent by Hell . . .   Un inviato dell' inferno io son . . .

MELITONE

I always said so . . .   L'ho sempre detto . . .

ALVARO

       Earth, gape and hide me,   Apriti, o terra,
And Heaven send your lightning . . .   M'ingoi l'inferno . . .
Receive me, O Hell . . .   Precipiti il ciel . . .
Let all creation perish . . .   Pera la razza umana . . .

(He climbs higher and throws himself into the void.)

ALL

Oh save him! . . . Almighty Lord . . .   Orrore! . . . Pietà Signor . . .
Misericordia!   Misericordia!

(All kneel.)

Final Curtain.

Discography by *Martin Hoyle*. For detailed analysis the enthusiast is referred to *Opera on Record*, ed. Alan Blyth, Hutchinson, 1979. The recordings here listed are in Italian.

Conductor Orchestra/Opera House	*Serafin* Scala	*Molinari-Pradelli* Sta Cecilia	*Previtali* Sta Cecilia	*Levine* LSO, Alldis Choir
Leonora	Callas	Tebaldi	Milanov	L. Price
Alvaro	Tucker	Del Monaco	Di Stefano	Domingo
Carlo	Tagliabue	Bastianini	Warren	Milnes
Padre Guardiano	Rossi-Lemeni	Siepi	Tozzi	Giaiotti
Melitone	Capecchi	Corena	Mantovani	Bacquier
Preziosilla	Nicolai	Simionato	Elias	Cossotto
Disc UK	SLS 5120	GOS 597	GOS 660	RLO 1864/4
Tape UK	TC-SLS 5120	–	–	RK 1864
Excerpts UK (disc)	–	SDD 292	–	
Disc US	3-Sera 688	Lon 1405	–	ARL4 1864
Tape US	–	–	–	ARK3 2543
Excerpts US (disc)	–	Lon 25085	–	ARS1 1883
Excerpts US (tape)	–	–	–	ARK1 1883

Bibliography

The Force of Destiny is the last opera covered by Julian Budden in the second volume of his classic study *The Operas of Verdi* (London, 1978). This chapter contains an exceptional amount of detailed observation, original documentation and lively commentary even by the high standard of these books.

Aspects of the opera are the subject of many essays in the Bulletins Nos. 4-6 of the Istituto di Studii Verdiani (1961-5), all of which are translated into English. These include character studies of Leonora, Don Carlos, Preziosilla and Melitone, as well as an essay by Winton Dean on the echoes of Donizetti in Verdi operas.

It is obviously mentioned in all the other biographies of the composer (for instance, Francis Toye 1931, Frank Walker 1962) and the important letters which Verdi wrote at the time of the composition are contained in Charles Osborne's translation of them (Gollancz, 1971). Other contemporary sources and beautiful illustrations may be found in William Weaver's *Verdi: A Documentary Study* (Thames & Hudson, 1977). Gabriele Baldini's *The Story of Giuseppe Verdi* is available in an English translation by Roger Parker (Cambridge, 1980), but unfortunately stops short of a full treatment of this opera.

The Spanish play is not available in English translation. A review of all the major criticism on *Don Alvaro* can be found in *Historia de la literatura española* by J.L. Alborg (Vol IV), (Madrid, 1980). The best single article is by Richard Cardwell in *Studies in Romanticism 12, 1973*: 'Don Alvaro or The Force of Cosmic Injustice'.

Schiller's *Wallenstein's Camp* was published by Penguin Books in 1979, translated by F.J. Lamport.

Contributors

Peter Conrad teaches English at Christ Church, Oxford. Among his books is *Romantic Opera and Literary Form* (University of California Press, 1977).

Richard Bernas is a conductor and musician actively involved in contemporary music. This has not prevented him from sustaining a lifelong enthusiasm for the works of Verdi and opera in general.

Bruce A. Brown presented the original version of his article in this book for a seminar at the University of California, Berkeley, and is currently working for his Ph.D. on the opéras-comiques of Gluck.

Andrew Porter, translator of many Verdi and Mozart operas as well as *The Ring* and *Tristan and Isolde*, is music critic for *The New Yorker*.